STEPPING-STONE MIRACLES

MIRACLES
(2nd Edition)

Published by Crossbridge Books, Worcester
www.crossbridgeeducational.com
© Crossbridge Books 2025

First published 2004

ISBN 978-1-916945-27-2

British Library Cataloguing in Publication Data.
A catalogue record for this book is available from
the British Library.

STEPPING-STONE
MIRACLES

(2nd Edition)

DES MORTON

(1933 – 2021)

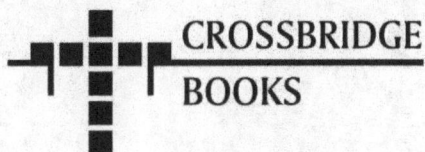

CROSSBRIDGE
BOOKS

PREFACE

I would like to thank the members of my family, who persistently encouraged me to put into writing some of the amazing occurrences that God has graciously seen fit to bless my life with. I felt that the best way to do this was to start at the beginning and tell it like it is; hence the autobiographical approach.

It is my heartfelt prayer that the Good Lord will use these simple testimonies of His miracle power, for His Glory.

I would like to express my heartfelt appreciation to the team of ministers, Elders, Deacons and church members who have faithfully supported me in the work of the ministry over the past thirty-seven years.

I want also, to say a grateful thank you to my secretary, Valerie Simpson, who has painstakingly translated my handwriting, produced beautiful typing and finished the manuscript.

Finally, I must express my unbounded gratitude to my dear wife Rosalie, for her unfailing love and support both in the ministry and in our many years of married life.

Des Morton
Elim Pentecostal Church
Keynsham
2004

DEDICATION

I dedicate this book to my dear friend,
the late Jim Douglas, who first
told me about Jesus.

FOREWORD

It is a privilege to be asked to write the foreword to "Stepping-stone Miracles", foremostly because God permitted me to have some part in Des Morton's conversion to Christ. Needless to say I have watched his own spiritual growth with much joy. I have also seen, with much gratitude to God, the way in which He has used Des, not only in Keynsham but much further afield. In these pages you will see, yet again, how God is able to take someone who has given over their life to Christ and give it the direction He plans for it and, at the same time, cause it to bring blessing to others.

A number of years ago I conducted the pioneer crusade in the Keynsham Co-operative Hall. From nineteen people in a hired hall to a super church building with 200 people is a miracle in itself. This is exactly what God has done during the more than 30 years that Des has been the Pastor of the Elim Pentecostal Church in Keynsham.

This is an inspiring story of hard work, true commitment and faithful ministry which has resulted in the triumph of faith and underlines the truth that we too can witness the miraculous, not only in the big events in life but also in the small, everyday events as we are prepared to open up our lives to God in simple faith.

As you read this book you will be encouraged, inspired and blessed. I certainly was.

RON JONES
(Former General Superintendent of the
Elim Pentecostal Churches)

Contents

1

Beginnings

As I gazed in amazement at the shining figure standing at the foot of my bed, I instinctively knew that I was looking at an angel.

It was one of those one-off, wonderful interventions of God that have periodically encouraged me along life's way, leaving an indelible impression upon my mind and heart.

This vision of an angel, which took place one winter's night as I awoke from sleep, opened my understanding of the 'spirit world' about us and sent me plunging into weeks of study on the subject.

However, I rush ahead of myself! Let me first of all say, it has been my personal experience and is indeed my belief, that the miraculous working of God in individual believers' lives, comes to each of us like a series of 'stepping-stones' bringing us safely through to the next stage of our earthly journey.

Perhaps months, or even years, may elapse between each 'miracle stone' and the next, and often it seems that we will never make it — then suddenly, something happens from God and there it is — for us to stand upon.

❦❦❦❦❦❦❦❦❦❦❦❦❦❦❦❦❦❦❦❦❦❦❦

I was born into a family where such things sometimes happened. It has been said, "Miracles happen to those who believe in them" — well, my family certainly believed in them.

My maternal grandfather, Tom Green, was a rough, tough, Kingswood miner, who was wonderfully converted to Christ in an evangelistic tent mission, around the time of the Welsh revival, in the early years of the 20th century.

The conversion of Tom Green was itself an outstanding miracle of grace. Tom's life was rough, crude and very hard. He started work in the pit at the age of eleven and worked there for over forty years. Then, on retiring from the pit, he worked as a docker, unloading goods at the Bristol docks.

His younger years consisted of one continual round of beer, gambling and street fighting. Tom was immensely strong and fit and was, in his eyes, an athlete. Indeed, he would often enter the local athletic races and beat all comers. He was known to jibe at the entrants and mock them for "sucking lemons" at the beginning of a race — whereupon he would then down a pint of beer and simply win the race.

One day a united church gospel crusade opened in Kingswood in the old preaching grounds of George Whitefield and John Wesley. My grandmother Emily attended, and as she listened to the preacher, gave her heart to Christ. The first stepping-stone was now in my family.

That night as she returned home, she found her husband gambling and drinking with his cronies. With a fiery glint in her eye, she told Tom what she had done and said that he was to come with her the next day.

"What!" roared Tom, "I'm not going to a place like that, with all those Holy Joes."

But next evening, to the amazement of his mates, Tom did go with his determined wife. My grandfather told me, as soon as he set foot inside the large tent that was packed with singing

❦❦❦❦❦❦❦❦❦❦❦❦❦❦❦❦❦❦❦❦❦❦❦

people, he felt God's presence.

The preacher, a Rev. Penfold from the United States of America, preached that night on the text, "My Spirit will not contend with man for ever" (Genesis 6:3). Tom said he knew it was "now or never", and with a repentant heart and tear-stained face, went forward, knelt at the front with other new converts and committed his life to Christ.

The change in Tom Green's life was sudden and dramatic. He immediately stopped all swearing and coarse language, plus drinking and gambling. He went into work the next day, rolled his sleeves up showing his rippling muscles and said, "Men, I got converted last night and from now on I don't want to hear any more cursing and swearing in my presence" — and from that day, no man ever used bad language in his vicinity.

He later joined the local Mission brass band and beat the big drum in the open-air meetings.

Having never attended school, he could not read or write; but he prayed about it, and with his wife's teaching, eventually learned to read.

As a young boy, I remember him many years later, reading the Bible and singing the old Sankey hymns by the fireside. His favourite song was:

> *At the cross, at the cross, where I first saw the light*
> *And the burden of my heart rolled away;*
> *It was there by faith I received my sight,*
> *And now I'm happy all the day.*

I remember, it used to embarrass me if I had friends visiting at the time. But I now know what he had.

Following his conversion in the big tent, Tom soon took his children to the meetings and all (with the exception of my mother, who was just a baby at the time) gave their hearts to

CHAPTER ONE

Christ. My mother's time would come many years later. Tom joined the Kingswood Wesleyan Methodist Church and served the Lord with all of his heart.

4

2

Miracles start happening

Living in the same house as my grandfather, I would often sit enthralled at the wonderful stories he would tell of his younger years — like the time he saw Buffalo Bill and his Wild West show on the Bristol downs; Queen Victoria on her diamond jubilee Bristol visit; or his trip to Manchester as a young fellow. All were wonderful to me; but none so wonderful as the night he had a dream and saw a future event unfold.

In the dream he saw himself working at the coalface, the very place he had been working that very day. To his horror, he saw the roof cave in on top of him — crushing him in the downfall. Awaking with a start, he told his wife the dream and refused to go in to work the next day. To miss a day's work in those days would be hardship indeed for a poor miner's family. The financial pressure was great, but he utterly refused to go in, saying he believed God had told him — through the dream — to stay at home.

Sure enough, that very day, at the coalface where he

had worked, there was a terrible roof cave-in, which would certainly have killed him.

My grandfather's conversion was a great challenge to me as a boy. He was not perfect, still rough and ready and often irritated by old age and deafness. But each morning and evening, he would have his half-hour or so prayer time, when he would pray aloud for his family. He would mention us all by name. Twice daily, we would hear our names brought to the throne of grace in prayer.

Today, over half a century later, my two brothers, sister and myself, are all Christians — though grandfather died before he ever saw it come to pass.

I was born in the old miner's cottage that I lived in as a boy with my grandfather. In fact, I was born in the same front room that my mother was born in. That was how it was done in those far-off days of 1933. My birth, however, nearly killed my mother, as I was ten pounds in weight.

The family doctor said that complications had set in and that my mother would die unless a dramatic change for the better took place in the next 48 hours.

On hearing the news, my grandmother Emily went outside the house into the backyard and, kneeling down on the cold stone slabs, humbly asked God to heal her daughter who had just given birth. Instantly, my mother was healed and delivered.

My mother was so overjoyed at being healed by God; she picked me up in her arms and presented me as a tiny baby to Him.

She prayed, "Oh God, thank You for healing me — I now give You my son. Please take him and when he grows up, use him to preach Your goodness."

Twenty-two years were to pass, and then one September Sunday night in 1955, I came home and told her: "Mum, I got

❦❦❦❦❦❦❦❦❦❦❦❦❦❦❦❦❦❦❦❦❦❦❦❦❦

converted tonight."

She replied, "That's right my son, just like your grandfather."

She had said nothing to me of what she had said to God at my birth, but at my announcement, the bell of remembrance rang in her heart and it all came flooding back to her: what she had said and done those twenty-two years earlier.

It was with great interest that she watched my developing Christian life and she waited to see what would happen. It came about when she heard me preach my first sermon, that she described what had taken place at my birth and how God had taken her at her word.

My mother Ella Louisa, though a nominal believer in God and Christ, had never actually committed her life to Christ. As mentioned, she, being the youngest member of the family in the early days — at the conversion of her father — got left behind somehow, being just a baby. But, being brought up in a Christian home, she instinctively prayed for her needs.

One day, when she was just a young teenager, her mother Emily, my grandmother, was taken ill and was confined to bed. They were both alone in the house. During this time, her mother needed to be lifted out of bed to be relieved; so the slim slip of a girl fell upon her knees and prayed. She simply asked God for strength to tend her mother's needs.

She testified that as soon as she made the request, a strange power came into both her hands; they felt like two lead weights, which she could hardly raise. Trembling with excitement, she slid her hands underneath her mother's body (who was a large woman) and lifted her as if she was just a piece of paper — no weight at all. After her mother's needs had been attended to, she quietly lifted her back into her bed and the power left her hands. For a brief moment of time, my mother as a young girl had received a 'Samson experience'

❦❦❦❦❦❦❦❦❦❦❦❦❦❦❦❦❦❦❦❦❦❦

from God. (Judges 14:6.)

My mother had a generally sad life, being widowed at the age of thirty-nine, after only fourteen years of marriage. She was left with four children to bring up — and times were hard in those days.

I am glad to say though, some six months after my conversion at the age of twenty-two, my mother committed her life to Christ and God's joy filled her aching heart. There was however, a further deep-rooted need still to be dealt with in her life.

Demonic deliverance

All through her life, my mother had been somewhat 'psychic' and prone to seeing spirit beings in the night.

It all stemmed from when, as a very young girl, perhaps only six or seven years of age, she called to a neighbour's house and, glancing in at the window, saw an elf-like creature dancing in the front room beckoning her to come in.

She knocked at the door of the house and asked if she could possibly play with the little girl dancing in the front room. She was promptly told that there were no children in the home. 'Spirit' visions plagued her from that day onward until she came to Christ.

At her conversion, the visions ceased. However, the deep need for full deliverance did not occur until some months later when I arrived home from church late one Sunday night.

I saw my mother in the armchair looking very depressed — she had been too depressed to attend the service and did not know why. I automatically put my arm around her and just prayed over her.

"Lord," I prayed, "please bless my mother and lift this evil depression from her — in the name of Jesus. Amen."

Immediately, the deliverance began to take place. The effect was staggering and took both of us completely by surprise. Suddenly, my dear mother started to vomit evil presences from within her. Like dark patches of blackness, evil spirits that had been deep rooted for many years, started to be ejected and came out one at a time.

My mother wept for joy and we gave thanks to God. Her old problem — which she could not previously understand — was gone forever.

All hail the power of Jesus' Name,
Let angels prostrate fall.
Bring forth the royal diadem
And crown Him Lord of all.

3

Voice in the night

I was converted to Christ in September 1955 — brought to the Saviour through the faithful witness of an office colleague, who became a good friend and co-worker in the gospel — Jim Douglas.

My personal journey, however, began some months earlier on the Good Friday of that same year. I had been invited by a neighbour to watch a special television broadcast from the Kelvin Hall, Glasgow and to hear the renowned American evangelist, Dr Billy Graham.

The novelty of watching television (which was rare in those days) and hearing this famous preacher, whose great London crusade the previous year had been nationwide news, attracted me. So that afternoon, with other members of my family, we went to watch this historic event. Never before, or since, to date, has such an evangelistic event ever been broadcast throughout the country on BBC nationwide television. I had no idea that gospel history was in the making, or indeed the effect
it was to have on my life.

❧❧❧❧❧❧❧❧❧❧❧❧❧❧❧❧❧❧❧❧❧❧

Almost half a century has passed since that particular Good Friday broadcast, but the wonderful crusade service is still indelibly fixed in my memory.

I vividly remember Cliff Burrows leading the singing of a large choir before thousands of people in the great arena. The gospel singer was George Beverly Shea and I recall being quite stirred as he sang in his rich baritone voice — *"Were you there when they crucified my Lord?"*

Later in the service, Billy Graham stood up and spoke to the nation on the 'Crucifixion of Christ'. His text was: *"But God forbid that I should glory, save in the cross of our Lord Jesus Christ"* (Galatians 6:14 [KJV]). As he preached, I became aware of being drawn to the cross, like a pin drawn to a magnet. I did not know then, that Jesus had said, *"But I, when I am lifted up from the earth, will draw all men to Myself"* (John 12:32). This I certainly began to experience that day in our neighbour's living-room.

At the conclusion of his message, Dr Graham then invited the people to respond and commit their lives to Christ. As we watched, we saw hundreds stream forward to the front, to do just that. Dr Graham then turned to the viewers and invited them to make a similar commitment, by kneeling in their living-rooms and surrendering their lives to Christ. It was at that point I found myself rebelling and resisting this 'emotional appeal' and I walked out of the room — turning my back on the gospel invitation.

A short time later, whilst doing my usual weight-training workout in the gym, a startling thing occurred. As I was performing a heavy exercise called 'press-on-bench', in which lying flat on my back, I would press a barbell of 240 lbs to arms' length — suddenly all the strength went out of my left wrist and the barbell came crashing down across my throat — embedding my Adam's apple into the back of my neck.

❦❦❦❦❦❦❦❦❦❦❦❦❦❦❦❦❦❦❦❦❦❦

Blue flashes shot before my eyes as I fought for breath and a terrifying thought gripped my mind — "I'm dying — where will I go? — It certainly won't be to heaven, because I said 'no' to Billy Graham when he invited me to surrender to Christ — so it must be to the other place."

Fear filled my heart — but at that point, my training partner dashed forward, grabbed the barbell and lifted it from my throat. At the same time, he hit the back of my neck, dislodging my Adam's apple that was stuck — and I began to breathe freely again. It was an experience that I would never, ever forget and a major stepping-stone in my personal journey to Christ.

Not long after this 'breaking down' experience, I moved to a different office in the firm where I worked, and met Jim Douglas. Almost from the word 'go', he began to talk about the Lord Jesus Christ, as someone who really knew Him, and we were often engaged in long conversations.

After several months of being witnessed to concerning the claims of Christ, and after much persuasion, I accepted an invitation to attend the City Temple, Bristol, with both Jim and his wife Pauline.

As soon as I entered the large modern building, I couldn't help noticing that it was packed with hundreds of people, with chairs down the aisles to get more people in. The meeting was vibrant with singing and praise and alive with what I now know to have been a 'Revival' atmosphere.

The Pastor, Rev. Ron Jones, preached that night on the story of the cross, which he entitled "The Slain Way." That night God spoke to my heart and I surrendered my life to Christ.

I had experienced quite a powerful conversion, when for the first time in my life I felt the presence of God — like my grandfather before me. I wept like a baby as I knelt at the

❧❧❧❧❧❧❧❧❧❧❧❧❧❧❧❧❧❧❧❧❧❧❧

communion table before some five hundred people. From that point on, my life completely changed, as the God I had always believed in came into my life.

I discovered later that a certain young lady, who saw me go forward in the meeting; turned to her sister and said: "That's the young man I'm going to marry." Her name was Rosalie — and she did indeed become my wife; at the time of writing — married for forty-five years.

Splash!

My first actual contact with Rosalie was on the occasion of my baptism by total immersion, the following month.

In those far-off days of the 1950s I had a shock of thick fair hair, and when I was immersed in the City Temple baptismal pool, my soaked head came out full of water. Instinctively, I shook my head, and with a sharp jerk a sheet of water shot out, hitting a young lady sitting in the front row. Yes … it was Rosalie!

Soon afterwards, that baptismal splash became the point of contact whereby we became friends, which developed into courtship and eventually, two years later — to marriage. Someone said that I had "married the prettiest girl in Redfield".

Rosalie was not only very attractive. with her dark hair, green eyes and well cut features, but she was also a very committed Christian; having been converted three years earlier in the mighty pioneer crusade in the Colston Hall, Bristol, led by Rev.'s P.S. Brewster and Willard Cantelon. It was this evangelistic mission that had founded and established the Elim City Temple in the city.

I have long since realised that God had chosen the ideal wife as my helpmeet for the ministry.

❦❦❦❦❦❦❦❦❦❦❦❦❦❦❦❦❦❦❦❦❦

The visit

In the immediate few days that followed my conversion (as sometimes does happen to young converts) I began to doubt the reality of it all. I had told my family that I had found Christ and witnessed to my colleagues in the office where I worked to that effect; yet, by the time the following Sunday came around, exactly one week later, I began to ask myself — 'did I imagine it?'

I attended the Sunday services with Jim and Pauline and really enjoyed the lively Pentecostal meetings, but still these thoughts of doubt niggled at me.

That Sunday night I went to bed with a host of thoughts and queries racing through my mind ... Was the Bible true? ... Is there a God? ... Did Jesus really die and rise again? ... Am I really saved? ... Have I been conned?

Gradually, I drifted off to sleep. Then suddenly, I was awake and afraid to open my eyes. I had awakened in the night and I knew God was in the room. His Holy presence, that I had felt a week prior, was upon me again — *only more so!* Like molten electricity, the power of God began to course through my body, causing both me and the bed to shake. All doubts about the reality of God immediately flew out the window and there I was, trembling in total belief.

Petrified, I managed to whisper, "O Lord, take it away; I'll never doubt you again; Lord I am afraid."

The Bible says, "The fear [healthy respect] of the Lord is the beginning of wisdom" (Psalm 111:10). I tasted that healthy reverence and respect that night.

But that was not all. As I lay quaking in the sheets — afraid to open my eyes in case of what I might see, I heard a gentle, audible whisper in my right ear from heavenly lips —

15

which simply said: "Holy, holy" — "Holy, holy" — "Holy, holy." These words were repeated over and over several times, after which, I somehow drifted off to sleep.

When I awoke, the presence of God was still in the room and His gracious anointing still upon me. Later, I discovered in the scriptures that the words I had heard, "Holy, holy" — "Holy, holy" — "Holy, holy" were what angelic beings say around the throne in heaven. (Isaiah 6:3; Revelation 4:8.)

Next day at work, I could not wait to inform my friend Jim of my experience. He looked at me strangely and then said, "Des, I think the Lord may be calling you to the ministry."

I replied, "Oh no, I don't think so," and pushed the idea from my mind.

However, from that point on, I began to sense God's call upon my life, and things certainly began to develop in that direction.

4

'The King's Messengers'

Eight months after I came to faith in Christ, God graciously baptised me with the Holy Spirit. This blessed experience took place in a 'seeking meeting' after the close of a Friday night prayer meeting at the City Temple, Bristol.

Pastor Ron Jones invited those who were seeking the initial filling of the Holy Spirit to remain behind for special prayer. The meeting really took off in prayer and worship to the Saviour, and after the Pastor had laid his hands upon the seekers, some began to be filled with the Spirit and exhibit speaking with 'tongues' as in Acts chapter two.

During this prayer time I personally experienced nothing, although two brethren, one on either side of me, began to joyfully worship in other tongues as the Spirit gave them utterance.

However, as the Pastor called the meeting to a close, and was in the process of talking to everyone, suddenly, the Holy Spirit fell on me like liquid fire and began to flow through me like a mighty river. Immediately, I also began to speak and

❧❧❧❧❧❧❧❧❧❧❧❧❧❧❧❧❧❧❧❧❧❧❧

worship the Lord in a language I had never learned. It was as if a string had been cut in my tongue and the wonderful freedom of a heavenly language began to flow from me. So powerful and wonderful was the experience, I felt that I didn't want to lose it; so all the way home, even on the bus, I was worshipping in tongues. My girlfriend, Rosalie, (now my wife) had to keep telling me to be quiet.

When I got home that night, I was still speaking with the tongues of the Spirit. My two younger brothers, Leslie and Gerald, who slept in the same cottage bedroom, woke up with a frightened start, thinking that a Red Indian was in the room! Soon, I noticed that a new power had entered my life — power to witness and also to preach.

Shortly afterwards, I was asked to give a short testimony of salvation at a local Baptist church one Sunday. In response, I had written out the five-minute testimony on a piece of card, but when I arose to speak, I completely forgot all about my notes and started to preach the gospel.

My friend Jim said, "Des, I didn't know you could preach."

"Neither did I," was my reply.

Jim's father, a godly Apostolic Pastor, asked me to preach at his church. So, in company with his two sons, Jim and Richard, and also his church pianist Clem, we met for prayer one Tuesday night and to practise some songs for the forthcoming meeting. God really blessed in the Sunday service and soon we were invited to conduct other evangelistic meetings in the city. Souls were being saved in almost every meeting we took.

We continued to meet regularly for prayer. It was in one such meeting that, as we were all kneeling in prayer, God's spirit moved mightily upon us, resulting in Pastor Douglas prophesying, that from henceforth, the team was to be called: 'King's Messengers'. Thus the 'King's Messengers' —

Pentecostal, musical evangelists — were born.

For the ensuing eight years, we travelled the country in many towns, villages and cities, conducting weekend missions. The original team of Christian businessmen changed shape slightly over the years, but settled with Jim and Richard Douglas, George Lancaster, Graham Britton and myself.

The team presented a variety of gospel music with varied instruments including trumpets, guitars, trombone, violin and piano, and quartet, duet and solo singing. In addition, Richard, a clever artist, would paint a beautiful scenic oil painting in just fifteen minutes, whilst the meeting was in progress. This was then given away to the person bringing the most first-time visitors to the mission.

In those far-off days of the 1950s and 60s, this worked very successfully, resulting in many souls being saved. We would conduct meetings for all denominations, including 'Youth for Christ'. Often we would leave on a Friday evening and return in the early hours of Monday morning, then get up for work. I thank God for those eight years of incessant evangelism, which resulted in hundreds of precious souls being won for Christ. It was this very practical training ground that God used to prepare me for the ministry.

Yellow tie

On one of our weekend gospel excursions in the early 1960s, we were invited to join Canadian evangelist Dr John Wesley White on his 'Ringing Worcester' crusade. He was in the process of completing a two-week evangelistic mission and had invited the 'King's Messengers' to provide 'musical messages' for the final weekend.

Dr White, a Billy Graham Associate Evangelist, was a

❧❧❧❧❧❧❧❧❧❧❧❧❧❧❧❧❧❧❧❧❧❧❧

dynamic and prolific preacher and drew large crowds to the meetings. On the last night of the united Church mission, which had been held in a number of halls and churches across town, the final rally was conducted in a huge Baptist church and was packed to capacity for the occasion.

We duly presented our gospel songs and musical items and were followed by Dr White, who rose to preach. However, even as he started his sermon, a small gang of teenagers entered the hall and clattered up the stairs to the balcony, squeezing in at the back. Their leader, a leather-jacketed youth of about eighteen years of age, who sported a bright yellow tie, was obviously intent on starting trouble right from the outset.

Sure enough, the youth started to make rude remarks about the preacher and his sermon, causing the rest of the group to break out laughing. This continued for about ten minutes or so, until at last, Dr White suddenly ceased from preaching and pointed up to the balcony, "Hey, you up there with the yellow tie," he shouted, "I believe you are as yellow as your tie!"

Everything went suddenly very quiet as the whole congregation turned to gaze at the young man with the yellow tie.

The teenager muttered something about "cutting him up with my blade afterwards", but the preacher was able to continue without further interruption.

We all wondered what was going to happen at the end of the meeting, but as Dr White began to give the appeal for sinners to come to Christ, who should be the first of a great crowd of new converts making their way to the front, but the troublesome teenager with the yellow tie — this time with tears in his eyes.

Dr White smiled, went down to the front to meet him and gave him a big 'gospel hug', welcoming him to the family of God.

Commenting afterwards, Dr White told us that he felt motivated by the Holy Spirit to take the action he did.

Fishers of men

I experienced a similar happening when we led an after-church 'fishing' meeting at Zion Chapel, Bedminster Bridge, Bristol.

The Pastor had organised the young people to go out 'fishing' in the coffee bars of Bedminster, inviting the young Teddy boys and Teddy girls (as they were called then), to come back to the church for free coffee, biscuits and music — we were the music.

About a dozen or so young people were 'fished in' that way, but they came in very noisy and became even louder when they found out that they had to wait until after they had heard a preacher, before they could receive their refreshments.

I remember Jim and Richard playing their trumpets as loudly as they could to drown the din. The noise seemed at fever pitch when at last, I rose to preach. I remember trying to preach a little gospel message entitled, "The Crushed Rose" — which focused on Christ 'the Rose of Sharon', being crucified and crushed on the cross of Calvary.

I had to speak very loudly for the first few sentences in an effort to be heard; amazingly, however, as soon as the cross was mentioned, the noise subsided. As I continued to describe the terrible sufferings of Christ on the cross, paying the price for our sins, they all went totally quiet.

Then, at the conclusion of the message, as I began to invite those who wished to take their stand at the cross and receive Christ as their Saviour, to come forward — nine, from the previously rowdy group, rose to their feet and came forward to

❀❀❀❀❀❀❀❀❀❀❀❀❀❀❀❀❀❀❀❀❀❀❀

stand in commitment before the congregation of other young people — weeping as they came.

After the meeting, others remained behind to talk about spiritual issues, which developed into an ongoing counselling session for all who came, with weekly follow-up Bible studies and fellowship meetings at the Minister's home on Thursday nights. There we met an unusual, tough group of young people from the local area, all wanting to find out more about the Bible.

One such young man was Reg, who had been the 'terror of Bedminster', but whose life had dramatically changed since recently finding Christ. Reg used to carry an open razor blade inserted in his peaked cap, so he could use it as a weapon to 'chip' people's faces when he removed his hat. Reg, however, had got truly 'saved' and had become a new creature in Christ, overnight.

It was a joy to fellowship with both him and his girlfriend in those weekly meetings. We thrilled as we watched them grow in the things of God. Over the passage of time, however, as the 'King's Messengers' moved on to other ministries, we lost touch with them.

Some years later, whilst I was browsing in the local Bristol Bible shop at Park Street, who should come into the shop but Reg and his girlfriend — now his wife. Not only had they been married for some time, but also, Reg had graduated from Bible College and was serving the Lord in the church ministry. Even his accent and his speech had changed. The ways of God are past finding out!

As the 'King's Messengers' developed under God, the memory is filled with thrilling accounts of missions and rallies at cities and towns throughout the country — in such places as Birmingham, Manchester, Dagenham, Exeter, Gloucester, Salisbury, Yeovil, Bridgwater, Redruth, Torquay and a host more.

In the 1970s, the team expanded further with the inclusion of three Christian businessmen: Mervyn Douglas, Jim Elmer and Steve Lewis. Today, Mervyn and Jim are Pastors of flourishing churches and Steve is a director of large evangelistic youth rallies.

The 'King's Messengers' continued in various forms and still continues to operate from time to time, with second and third generations from the original members. I still call myself a 'King's Messenger'.

★★★★

5

The Keynsham Call

I was inducted as Pastor of the Elim Pentecostal Church, Keynsham, Bristol, on 14th April 1966. I was 32 years of age and the occasion is still crystal clear in my memory, because we had a freak blizzard at the time and there were deep snowdrifts everywhere.

The old 'tin mission' was full for the occasion with support from my home church, the City Temple, Bristol. However, after the induction service was over, the congregation soon reverted to its original nineteen members. Little did I know though, that I was embarking on a new series of stepping-stone miracles that would follow me right through the ministry.

Looking back, I see His abundant provision. God has seen fit to graciously bless me with many providential occurrences that have brought me from stepping-stone to stepping-stone along life's way. You don't have to be a great world evangelist, or the minister of a mega church to see such miracles happen. The miracle-working God is with every born-again Pastor, whether he is the minister of a large or small church.

❦❦❦❦❦❦❦❦❦❦❦❦❦❦❦❦❦❦❦❦❦

In my case, I became the Pastor of a small church, in a small town.

After about twelve years, the congregation had built up to some seventy members. It had been extremely hard going for the first ten of those years; I had to work at a secular job — both full time and part time, in order to support my family.

Eventually, in 1976, I was able to pastor the church full time, and for a while, things got easier. Then I started to experience problems in the ministry, plus pressures of personal financial need. My car also was literally falling to pieces, and as we lived six miles from the Keynsham church, a car was an absolute necessity.

Such was the difficulty of the situation that I began to ask myself the question 'was my ministry now coming to a close at Keynsham?' 'Was it now time for me to seek a move to another church?' In fact, a couple of years previously, I had been invited to accept another Pastorate but had declined. Now, I was beginning to re-think my situation. After all, I thought, most ministers I know stay in churches only five years or so, and then move on. I had been at my church for eleven years; perhaps it was God telling me that it was now my time to relocate.

The very day all this was going through my mind, the telephone rang. It was the Rev. Ron Jones, now General Superintendent of the Elim movement.

"Des," he said, "have you ever thought of moving from Keynsham?"

I readily replied, "Funny you should ask that, for I have been pondering that very thought."

Then he explained that because of various retirements in the ministry, three large churches had vacancies for mature, experienced Pastors and that my name had been mentioned for possibly one of them. However, he pointed out, he had to have my answer in three days. I assured him that I would telephone him on the morning of the fourth day with my answer.

Excitedly, I told my wife Rosalie of the invitation and said I felt that God might be opening a new door for ministry. We both agreed that we would tell no one but God and wait for His answer; with this added proviso, that if we did not hear from God in the allotted three days, then we would take it that God meant us to accept one of these churches — and I had one in mind. But if He wanted us to stay, He must tell us directly and clearly and also meet the need of my old car.

The three days passed uneventfully and I was already making mental preparation for the move.

When the morning of the fourth day arrived, I was thinking what to say to Pastor Jones when a letter addressed to me came through the letterbox. It was from a Christian farmer and his wife, whom I had only met two or three times previously. They were godly Christian folk and people of prayer.

In the letter they told me that they had been in prayer and felt strongly led by God to write to me saying that God would not have me move from Keynsham. They went on to say that I was God's man for Keynsham and that I must not think of moving away. They ended their little letter by saying that they had enclosed a cheque for £2,000 — to be used for whatever need I had.

To say that I was completely bowled over by this letter and contents would be radically understating the case. God had done exactly what we had asked of Him. He had replied to our specific request in the required time limit and also provided £2,000.

My immediate reaction was to drive out to the farm and see these dear folk, which I did. I explained the situation and the prayer 'fleece' that we had placed before the Lord. They in turn were thrilled at the confirmation, through the leading of the Holy Spirit, in their lives. I then asked them what they wanted me to do with the cheque for £2,000.

They replied, "What's your car like?" — To which I

27

❀❀❀❀❀❀❀❀❀❀❀❀❀❀❀❀❀❀❀❀❀❀

answered, "Take a look and see."

When they saw the condition of my car, full of rust and on the way out, they responded by saying, "Put the money towards another car" — which I did!

Back in 1977, £2,000 was *two thousand pounds,* and I was able to purchase a brand new Ford 'Popular' 1100, taxed, insured and on the road for £1,950. With the £50 left over I was able to purchase a desperately needed desk for my study, which I am still using. Praise God.

The following Sunday morning, I informed the church of the events of the past week and God's wonderful intervention and provision. The congregation was both shocked and thrilled at what had happened. Shocked at the news that I had nearly left the church and thrilled that I was now staying — permanently.

I had told the church that I was now staying, come what may in the future. God had called me to Keynsham, eleven years after I had been there and I would continue until I could preach no more — or God told me to stop.

Since that time in 1977, we have seen the work at Keynsham flourish and grow under God's gracious hand. We now occupy a beautiful purpose-built church complex, which has become a training centre for evangelism and outreach. In addition, two branch churches have been established in the nearby areas of Kingswood and Brislington.

Gospel teams regularly conduct meetings throughout the U.K. and different parts of the world — including Africa, America and India.

TO GOD BE THE GLORY

6

'It's a boy!'

Very often, God's supernatural intervention occurs in times of great trial and stress. This was indeed the case with the birth of our babies in the 1960s.

My wife and I lost two babies a short while after birth. One baby was a beautiful little girl named 'Cherie', who died on my wife's lap at almost a month old. The second baby was a wonderful little boy named 'Darren', who died in hospital the day after he was born. The great grief of this double bereavement is hard to describe. Only those who have endured child loss will understand.

Somehow, however, with the Lord's gracious help and comfort, we pulled through. A scripture verse from the apostle Paul's letter to the Roman Christians, was a great source of encouragement to us at that time — and I might add, still is:

"And we know that in all things God works for the good of those who love Him, who have been called according to His purpose" (Romans 8:28).

29

❀❀❀❀❀❀❀❀❀❀❀❀❀❀❀❀❀❀❀❀❀❀❀

We claimed that promise by faith, applying it to our deep need; believing that God would use even the bad things to work together for our good.

It took time, but that is exactly what He did; also in the process, enabling us to counsel and comfort from personal experience those who have gone through similar tragedy. We also know that in the "sweet by and by" we will have two children to welcome us home, and renew fellowship together.

At times we wonder if they will still be babies in heaven, or will they have grown up having being tutored by the angels? Either way, it will certainly be interesting to find out.

DAVID

In 1967, we met a famous London geneticist who counselled us as to whether a third pregnancy should be considered. The specialist informed us that normally, the chances of a baby being born with heart problems, (which was what our babies suffered with) was one in a hundred. He then further explained that should this occur, the chances of it happening a second time, was reduced to one in fifty. This was also our experience. He then drew a family chart and said, the chances of it happening a third time were now reduced even further to one in ten — but still felt the odds were favourable. To me it felt like bookmaking on Derby Day.

When we returned home and after a serious discussion, we decided we would try for one further pregnancy and place the matter in God's hands. I remember saying to Rosalie that I would only pray the once during this attempt, because God was not deaf. Thus Rosalie became pregnant with our third child.

Eight months into the pregnancy, our family doctor examined Rosalie and said that this baby was going to be very

❦❦❦❦❦❦❦❦❦❦❦❦❦❦❦❦❦❦❦❦❦❦

small indeed, even smaller than our previous two children; their weights being just 6lb 7oz and 5lb 8oz.

A few weeks later, Rosalie began to experience further problems and was confined to hospital prior to birth time. She always experienced difficulty in bringing forth children, putting great pressure upon the babies' hearts. Such was the case this third time.

With a heavy heart, I arrived at Southmead Hospital, Bristol, for visiting time. The child had not yet been born and Rosalie was suffering extended labour again. I remember arriving in our old Ford Popular car and pulling up at the hospital a little early. It was then that I lifted my heart in prayer for the first time since I had prayed at the commencement. Actually, it was more of a 'cry' than a prayer. Closing my eyes in the old car, I exclaimed: ***"O Lord, what is happening?"***

What followed then took me completely by surprise. Suddenly, the mighty presence of God entered the car. The Holy Spirit filled me and the car; so much so, I felt we both might burst.

Then I heard a beautiful voice speaking clearly within my stomach saying, ***"Des — Jesus is here, all things are possible — only believe."***

Dazed at what was taking place, I began to shout and magnify the name of Jesus.

Coming to myself, I jumped out of the car and ran into the hospital ward. I caught sight of Rosalie languishing on her bed in great discomfort with a medical drip in her arm and a very worried look on her face. Rushing to her I said, "Rosalie, it's going to be alright this time — God has just spoken to me."

At my spoken word, in spite of all that was happening to her at that moment, Rosalie also believed and we rejoiced together. Later, after a prayer of thanksgiving, I left for home.

❀❀❀❀❀❀❀❀❀❀❀❀❀❀❀❀❀❀❀❀❀❀

Shortly afterwards, the doctors came to my wife and said that the baby's heart within the womb was getting weak and they were thinking of a caesarean operation; to which Rosalie replied, "I believe everything is going to be alright."

At work the following day, I received a phone call to go right away to the hospital. I rushed to Southmead Hospital as fast as I could, but told God en route that I believed His word. When I arrived at the ward entrance and asked to see my wife, the nurse asked, "Would you like to see your baby son first?"

In an utter daze, I was taken to the delivery room and there saw baby David. My first question was, "Is his heart alright?"

"Yes," was the reply, "as sound as a bell, and he is 8lb 4oz in weight."

My heart literally sang for joy as I went to see my wife, who was just recovering from the caesarean operation and still a little sleepy.

She awoke to see me smiling by her bedside with the news: "It's a boy — and his heart is fine!"

Rejoicing, we knew that we were the recipients of a great miracle.

All that happened over thirty years ago, and David is Assistant Pastor in our Team Ministry. In addition, with his lovely wife Elaine, they have presented us with three beautiful grandchildren — two boys and a girl. Their names are Zach, Martha and Joel respectively.

"The Lord has done this and it is marvellous in our eyes." (Psalm 118:23.)

God's mighty hand is at work behind the scenes. He does work things out for our good and His Glory! ***Hallelujah!***

I can't, however, let the occasion pass without mentioning David's contribution to a particular church service when he was just two and half years old.

It was Christmas time and I had just begun preaching a

seasonal sermon during the Sunday evening Carol Service, entitled: "Christmas in a Nutshell". I started by saying:

"There is nothing that I like more at Christmas time, than sitting down by a warm fire with a large dish of assorted nuts — walnuts — Brazil nuts — Spanish nuts — " I got no further, for suddenly a child's voice popped up and shouted:

"DOUGHNUTS!"

Everyone knew it was the minister's son and the entire congregation collapsed in laughter, completely stealing my thunder. Since that time, David has popped up in many services, but this time preaching his own sermons!

7

Heart to heart

In the summer of 1980, my brother Leslie, a Christian property developer, suffered a massive heart attack.

As the emergency ambulance sped him away to Frenchay Hospital, Bristol, his heart stopped beating en route, with the paramedics frantically trying to resuscitate him.

For a short while, they were successful; but as they entered the hospital gates, my brother sustained a second severe attack, which again stopped his heart.

It was while a team of doctors feverishly endeavoured to restore him, that I, and a small group of the family, including Leslie's pregnant wife Zynia, arrived on the scene. We were shunted into a side waiting room to await developments.

Immediately we began to call upon God in prayer; then my younger brother, Gerald, suggested we start praising the Lord in faith and thank Him for the answer. This we did and one can only wonder at what the rest of the hospital ward must have thought, with this collective noise coming out of the waiting room.

꽃꽃꽃꽃꽃꽃꽃꽃꽃꽃꽃꽃꽃꽃꽃꽃꽃꽃꽃꽃꽃

I hasten to add that, back at Keynsham, a dedicated group of prayer warriors met at the church and were also interceding in prayer for Leslie.

Eventually, a doctor in a long white coat and an even longer face, entered the waiting room and beckoned me over to him. At first, I thought he was going to tell us to keep the noise down, as this was a hospital. However, as I approached, I knew he had disturbing news.

"Mr Morton," he said, "I can't paint a blacker picture. We have managed to resuscitate your brother, but although his heart is now beating again, he is totally unconscious and has sustained massive brain damage."

He went on to say: "Frankly, there is no hope of recovery; I have never seen anyone walk out of a ward after being starved of oxygen for so long."

The doctor then asked me to gently break the news to Leslie's wife and to prepare for the worst. As he turned to leave the room, I asked if it would be alright to see Leslie and pray for him. He nodded and pointed to the drawn curtain surrounding Leslie's bed.

As I entered within the curtain, I saw my brother with his eyes closed, unconscious and barely alive. I instinctively laid my hand on his forehead and found myself saying, "Leslie, in the name of Jesus — get better!"

Instantly he opened his eyes, looked at me and said: "Hello Des — what happened?"

I replied, "You've had a heart attack old chap."

"Oh! That's what it was," said Leslie. "Can I see Zynia?"

"Well, I'd better ask the doctor first," I retorted, "but first of all, I want to say, you can't die yet!"

"Why?" he replied with a twinkle in his eye.

"Because you have to build us a church!"

In fact, the foundations of our beautiful new building,

which Leslie was managing for us, had already been laid. Twenty-one years later, in 2001, the final third phase of the project was opened — all under my brother's expert management. We praise God for His great goodness.

Back in the ward, I opened the curtain and called out to the doctor, "He is asking to see his wife, is that okay?"

"What!" cried the doctor. "If nothing happens now in the next twenty-four hours, he will be alright."

A stir went around the whole ward and an elderly Methodist gentleman in the bed opposite raised his hand and said, "I would like some of that!"

I asked him what his problem was and he said that he had had two heart attacks and was afraid to go to sleep. In fact, he had not slept for three days. He asked me to pray for him, which I then did, beseeching God for His 'beloved sleep' (Psalm 127:2 KJV).

As I prayed for this dear Christian brother, another man, a few beds down the ward, raised his hand and said, "I'd like some of that!"

This man's name was also Leslie, Leslie Anderson, and he lived not far from us, at Staple Hill, Bristol. He also explained that he had received two heart attacks, with his heart stopping both times and was afraid to go to sleep.

He further explained that during his second attack, he actually had an out-of-body experience. He said, "I vividly remember sliding out of my body, rising above the bed and seeing doctors trying to get my heart going again."

He continued, "I then looked behind me and saw an inky blackness — it frightened me to death! So much so, I literally began to swim back into my body and then I opened my eyes. I have not slept for three days and I've been afraid to go to sleep ever since. Would you please pray for me!"

So, laying my hands upon his head, I asked the Lord to

❧❧❧❧❧❧❧❧❧❧❧❧❧❧❧❧❧❧❧❧❧❧

bless him also with a restful sleep. The next day, when I came into the hospital to visit my brother, who was now doing remarkably well, the two men that I had also prayed for had not long woken up after a good long sleep.

The second man, Leslie Anderson, raised his hand again as soon as he saw me and said, "I'd like some more of that — would you please bless me again!"

His wife Sheila was sitting by his bed and I told them that I could not bless anyone — only the Lord Jesus Christ could do that. I also went on to explain that the most important healing was the healing of the soul. This meant receiving Jesus as Saviour for the forgiveness of sins. I asked him, would he like to do that?

"Oh, yes please!" he replied.

It was then that his wife exclaimed, "Pastor Morton, I must tell you that I am an atheist. I don't believe in anything — but if you can help my husband, please help him."

Taking hold of her husband's hand, I led him in the sinner's prayer of commitment. As we prayed together, the wonderful presence of the Holy Spirit descended upon both of us. Out of one eye, I noticed that Leslie Anderson was quivering under the Holy Spirit with tears in his eyes; not only that, the heart monitor began to go 'bleep', 'bleep', 'bleep'. 'What have I done?' was my first thought — but all was well.

I gave Leslie a gospel of John, which he opened and laid across his chest. "I shall sleep well tonight Pastor," he said with a smile.

A few weeks later, in one of our Sunday night services at Keynsham, who should walk in, but Leslie Anderson, with his wife Sheila and young daughter Kerry. After the gospel sermon and evangelistic appeal, I was thrilled to see both Sheila and Kerry come forward to surrender their lives to Christ. Sheila looked up and said, "The penny has dropped,

Pastor," and we rejoiced together.

When God intervenes, tragedy turns to triumph. It is a fact, that you can't have a miracle without there first being a crisis. In the crisis, people cry out to God and it is in answer to prayer that God intervenes.

The heart ward at Frenchay had produced a whole row of crisis miracles — stepping-stones along life's way.

8

The miracle church

The story of our beautiful 300-seater church building complex at Keynsham is a wonderful 'stepping-stone' miracle in itself.

In 1979, starting with only £26 in the building fund, we decided as a fellowship, to take a definite step of faith and build ourselves a brand new church building alongside the then old building.

I met with the leading brethren of the fellowship one Sunday morning after the service; the idea being to discuss extending our current 100-seater prefabricated building, because of the problems in accommodating our growing congregation.

One of the men, himself a builder, said, "Pastor, why don't we build a new church in the car park?"

The suggestion seemed impossible, but gradually the idea took hold in our hearts and, after much prayerful discussion, we committed ourselves to a 'self-build' programme, with the proviso that we would refuse to take out any mortgage that would cripple the church trying to repay the debt.

Our covenant was to trust the Lord for the financial

❀❀❀❀❀❀❀❀❀❀❀❀❀❀❀❀❀❀❀❀❀

provision and that if it was His will — He would provide. We decided that we would build the church at the pace that the Lord provided — a stage at a time.

This is exactly how it worked out; taking us some five years, as the gifts of money for materials gradually came in. Our first gift effort yielded a total of £800, which enabled us to install the drains and inspection chambers — all below ground. It seemed after weeks of work, nothing was accomplished, because it was all out of sight.

The work, however, had commenced and under the management of my brother Leslie (now healed and back in action after his heart attack) and the sacrificial giving and hard work of the entire fellowship, the new building began to take shape.

I shall never forget those wonderful, far-off work parties and the sense and thrill of actually building for the future. Nor will I soon forget the arrival of the women, with the men, all wearing their gum boots and armed with garden rakes, to spread and smooth out the ready-mix concrete that arrived in huge mixer lorries. It was a sight to behold, raising the eyebrows of many a passer-by, as our band of enthusiastic labourers laid the massive concrete base.

Eventually, we came to the 'roof raising' weekend, which turned into the most hair-raising part of the project. It reminded me of an old Tarzan movie, with ladders on high, ropes dangling and dozens of people clambering up and down the scaffolding in an effort to position the large roof trusses.

Then came the fitting of hundreds of roof tiles — a professional roofer helped us with them and miraculously, no one was killed or injured in the whole exercise. I remember thinking at the time, 'Thank God the age of miracles has not passed.'

❧❧❧❧❧❧❧❧❧❧❧❧❧❧❧❧❧❧❧❧❧❧
Opening Day

The first phase, and the main Hall of Worship, was completed after five years, at a cost of only £38,000 due to great labour-saving costs and cut-price material deals. This was all fully paid for, free of mortgage debt.

Pastor Ron Jones, accompanied by the wonderful 'New Creation Singers' — also from the Bristol City Temple, officially opened the new building in 1985. The other preacher that weekend was Rev. Jack Hetzel, a lively preacher from Texas, U.S.A.

The local newspaper (The *Keynsham Chronicle*) in a major headline report, labelled us:

THE MIRACLE D.I.Y. CHURCH

Over 400 people crammed into the hall that amazing day. How they all got in was another miracle.

Five years later, we opened a second extension 'facility block' of offices, kitchen and vestry. In 2001, the final third phase was completed and opened, being a large two-storey building of church halls and youth rooms. Again, the whole complex was fully paid for by the gifts of God's people — with no outstanding debt. The total overall cost of the faith project was (approx) £180,000; however, the building was recently insured for £1 million.

We at Keynsham Elim readily confess, that this is "The Lord's doing, and it is marvellous in our eyes" (Psalm 118:23 KJV). He is indeed "Jehovah Jireh" — the Lord who provides. (Genesis 22:14.)

Over the years, since that first phase opening in 1985, miracles of salvation, healing and restoration have taken place, plus many weddings, funerals, infant dedications and baptisms.

❧❧❧❧❧❧❧❧❧❧❧❧❧❧❧❧❧❧❧❧❧❧

All this the brethren saw by faith that Sunday morning back in 1979, when they believed God for a 'NEW church'.

Back to the future

A no lesser miracle had begun to unfold a number of years before Pastor Ron Jones launched the original pioneer crusade for Elim in the town during 1957.

Back in the early 1950s, a godly prayer intercessor — Miss Mary Clothier — became a vital link in God's chain of events.

Miss Clothier was the local prayer representative in Keynsham for W.E.C. (World Evangelisation Crusade). Often she would organise prayer weekends at her large home in the town and sometimes, young people would sleep over and stay for the whole weekend.

One Sunday morning, as Miss Clothier came downstairs, the young people noticed that her face was as white as a sheet.

"What's the matter? Has anything happened?"

"Yes indeed," she replied. "God has shown me a vision; I saw it as clear as day. I saw a large church, with crowds of people pouring from it at Balmoral Road — where the disused American isolation hospital is."

She was referring to the empty group of galvanised metal buildings that the American army used to quarantine soldiers with infectious diseases during the Second World War.

"D'you know what?" she said excitedly, "I'm going to purchase that old set of buildings and turn it into an Evangelical Mission, to secure it in faith for the future and for the building that will one day come."

This she did, employing a church Pastor from Bristol, a Mr Evans from Princess Hall, who had been a carpenter years

❀❀❀❀❀❀❀❀❀❀❀❀❀❀❀❀❀❀❀❀❀❀

before. After several months, with great skill, he turned it into an attractive building that became known as the 'Evangelical Church', which brought much gospel blessing to the area.

One of our present-day elders, Steve Lewis, used to attend the children's 'Lifeboys'; and as a young Christian, I was also asked to give my testimony of salvation there. Neither Steve nor myself could see what the future held, but Miss Clothier did.

At a later date, the 'King's Messengers', the gospel team of Christian businessmen that I had become involved with, were also asked to conduct a gospel service there at Harvest Festival — I was the preacher on that day. I remember that there was great blessing and that it was a very thriving work indeed, run by a lovely group of spiritual people.

However, as the years passed, the local Council ordered that the old building be demolished and a new church constructed in its place. Unfortunately the little fellowship could not rise to this and offered it to Elim, on condition they built a new church on the site. Thus, in 1965, the Evangelical Church building and land was handed over to Elim for the gospel work to continue.

In 1966 I entered the ministry and in the April, was inducted as the new Pastor. That very same year we demolished the old building and erected a semi-prefabricated church building, seating a hundred people. It was considered a temporary measure for ten years, but it lasted to the year 2000, while we constructed our final building extension.

When Miss Clothier saw the new small 'L' shaped building, the first thing she said to me was, "This is not the church I saw in my vision — it was much taller and bigger!"

My reply was, "The church you saw, Miss Clothier, is still to be built."

Sadly, in the 1970s, Miss Mary Clothier went to be with her

45

Lord without ever seeing the fruition of her 'vision'. However, when the new hall of worship was opened in 1985, two Christian ladies — Miss Gwen Isaacs and Miss Ann Perritt, came to the celebration services.

It turned out that these two sisters in the Lord were among the original young people in the W.E.C. prayer weekends, years before. They both said how thrilled they were to attend the opening, because the new building was "exactly like the one Miss Clothier described in her vision." Both ladies testified to this before the church congregation and, at a later date, were personally interviewed and videoed, their story being recorded for posterity.

There is no doubt about it, that at Keynsham Elim, we are reaping where others have sown, but it is also a great thrill to know that we too are part of

"THE CHURCH OF THE VISION"

9

Jason and Heaven

The telephone rang loudly in the early hours of a dark December morning. Awaking from sleep, I heard a voice on the line say:

"Des — Jason has just died! Would you come and wake up his father and tell him?"

I had known Jason Britton all his short life of seventeen years and his parents, Graham and Marilyn, were personal friends of my wife and myself. Graham, his father, had also been a member of the 'King's Messengers' team; now he was a Christian businessman.

Jason had suffered throughout his life with cystic fibrosis, an incurable disease of the lungs. As a young lad, whilst attending our church at Keynsham, one Sunday he surrendered his life to Christ and became a wonderful Christian. My wife and I got to know Jason really well and often visited him in hospital while he was on his many visits for treatment.

He also used to request me to visit him at his home, so we could talk about the things of God and do short Bible studies on various subjects such as healing, the second coming of Christ and Heaven etc.

47

Sometimes we would especially pray for his healing, claiming such promises as Isaiah 53:5 *"And by His wounds we are healed"* and Mark 16:18: *"They will place their hands on sick people and they will get well"*.

Over the months Jason, however, gradually grew worse, and unless an outright miracle happened, it was obvious that he would die.

A few days before he died, he asked me to visit him at his home. We talked again about the glories of heaven and the believer's eternal future.

Heaven was a subject that I had recently studied in depth for a church teaching series, which lasted several weeks. So I was able to draw on the study material for Jason. The series title was: "The Christian's Life — After Death".

Jason was so interested and fascinated by this subject and so full of questions. It was as if he was on a time limit — for knowledge.

His eyes would light up as we studied the scripture passages together, as he saw that heaven was indeed a real place, more real even than earth, full of beauty and splendour.

On this particular occasion, though he had been suffering so terribly, he got out of his chair, fell on his knees and prayed, saying:

"Thank You God for Your great goodness and love to me. I love You, praise Your Name."

When I heard that, I remember thinking, "Well Satan, what do you think about that?"

Jason was indeed an amazing young Christian and his deep commitment so often challenged my own.

The day before he died, I visited him again and there, with Marilyn his mother, committed him to God's tender care. Graham, his father, so affected by grief, had already been given a sedative by the doctor to help him sleep. I then left,

❀❀❀❀❀❀❀❀❀❀❀❀❀❀❀❀❀❀❀❀❀❀

requesting to be immediately informed of any developments.

A peep into Heaven

Early next morning, the telephone rang, bringing the news that Jason had died and would I come and awaken his father who was still sleeping.

Dazed, I clambered out of bed, peeping through the curtains to see the blackness of the early morning. Instinctively, I knew that I was confronted with one of the hardest tasks of my life. The thought that weighed heavily upon me was, 'How can I possibly wake up a devoted father already grief stricken to the point of distraction and inform him that his teenage son has died?'

I dressed, climbed into my car and began to drive towards the bereaved home which was some twenty minutes away. As I drove, I began to call upon God to help me.

"Lord," I cried, "I've been in the ministry all these years and I don't know what to tell Graham — please show me what to say."

Immediately, a vision 'into' heaven appeared before my eyes. It was like watching a coloured movie screen with sound track.

As I looked, I was conscious of driving the car, going through traffic lights and mentally taking the correct road turns, but all the time watching with 'wide eyes' what was beginning to unfold in front of me.

I was conscious also, of the gentle blessing of the Holy Spirit as I saw so clearly two persons talking to one another. It was a side-on view of Jason, conversing with the Lord Jesus. Jason, I noticed, was smartly dressed in a modern suit and Jesus had on a long white robe — and I could hear what they

❧❧❧❧❧❧❧❧❧❧❧❧❧❧❧❧❧❧❧❧❧❧

were both saying.

"Jesus, why didn't you heal me?" asked Jason. "Des Morton said that if I claimed that scripture in Isaiah 53 *'By your wounds I am healed'* then I would be healed! Why wasn't I healed?"

The Lord smiled, nodded and said, "How do you feel now?"

"Alright," said Jason.

"Are you in any pain now?"

"No!"

"Can you breathe properly now?"

I saw Jason breathe deeply, smile and say, "Yes — I can."

Then the Lord raised His hand and said, "What do you think of My Father's house?"

"Wonderful!" Jason replied.

Smilingly, Jesus said: "Well then!"

The vision faded almost immediately and I found myself right outside the house. I sat in the car for a few minutes pondering on what had been revealed; then, I knew exactly what I had to tell Graham — that Jason was alive and well in heaven and that this was his 'eternal' healing.

It is true that God does perform healings down here on earth, which may give us life for a further period of years; but eventually, we all still have to die.

True lasting healing is when we go to be with Christ, which, as the apostle Paul stated, is *"better by far"* (Phil.1:23). The believer wins both ways. If the Lord heals him here on earth, he is healed for a few more years; but if he dies and goes to glory, he is healed forever. Hallelujah! Either way he wins.

Excitement welled up within me as I got out of the car and entered the home. The living-room was full of relatives and I was relieved to see that Graham was already awake and sitting at the table.

I noticed that someone had made him tea and toast, but he was looking forlornly past it, gazing into space.

Instinctively, I put my arm around him and said, "Graham, this is what the Lord has just shown me on the way over. I've seen Jason in heaven with Jesus." I then explained all that had happened in the last few minutes.

He looked up and said, "Des, did you actually see Jason with Jesus? Is it really so?"

"Yes," I replied, "and he is perfectly well now."

Graham breathed a deep sigh of relief, ate his piece of toast and drank his cup of tea.

EPILOGUE

The funeral for Jason was one of the most inspiring that I have ever attended. The large Bristol City Temple was filled to capacity with folk from all walks of life, including many doctors, nurses and personalities from local radio and television. Jason had touched so many lives through his illness and it was truly heart warming to see them come.

Three ministers shared in the service: Rev. Ron Jones, Rev. Jim Dick and myself. It was my privilege to deliver the address and include some of the thoughts from the 'vision' experience.

The service was recorded on audio cassette and since that day, hosts of copies have been requested from around the country and different parts of the world. Many recordings have been requested for hospices, which has brought hope and encouragement to scores of people on the verge of eternity.

❦❦❦❦❦❦❦❦❦❦❦❦❦❦❦❦❦❦❦❦❦❦

Dimension Heaven

One aspect of our previous studies together on heaven, that I know particularly blessed Jason, was the experience of the first Christian martyr, Stephen, just before his death by stoning in Acts Chapter 7:55-56.

The scripture says that, *"Stephen, full of the Holy Spirit, looked up to heaven and saw the glory of God, and Jesus standing at the right hand of God. 'Look,' he said, 'I see heaven open and the Son of Man standing at the right hand of God'."*

It would seem to indicate that heaven is another dimension, not far from any one of us; and at death, it opens up to receive the believer. Stephen caught sight of this prior to his death and cried out at the glory of it. He then died under a shower of cruel stones and the Bible says: *"he fell asleep"* (v. 60). One can imagine him closing his eyes and suddenly waking up in the glory he had just viewed.

The Bible teaches that heaven (God's abode) is another world; and in that world lies a beautiful heavenly country with a gleaming Holy City of gigantic proportions. Jesus called that city, *"My Father's house"* (John 14:2) — a house with many mansions. A heavenly metropolis populated with millions of saints and angels in great eternal joy.

Isaac Watts wrote:

There is a land of pure delight
Where saints immortal reign.
Infinite day excludes the night
And pleasures banish pain.

It was the anticipation of such a wonderful place that thrilled the young heart of Jason, and he loved to discuss it.

I count it a great privilege not only to have known Jason, but to have caught sight of him in that other dimension; that beautiful city, whose builder and maker is God.

10

Jesus in the room

George Whiting was an extraordinary man. He was highly intelligent, artistic and industrious.

Among his many accomplishments was that of being an author, poet, artist, sculptor, an eloquent speaker and a builder — having designed and actually built his own spacious bungalow with large swimming pool. He was also a father of four.

During the Second World War, George was taken prisoner by the Japanese in the Far East and incarcerated in the horror camp at Haroekoe Island, Java.

He wrote of his many experiences in a harrowing, but highly informative book entitled *Japanese Bondage*, which was readily published. George also wrote a collection of poems, sonnets and limericks, graphically describing his days in the P.O.W. camp.

He emerged from his wartime experiences somewhat agnostic regarding the Bible view of God, but believing there was a supreme intelligence somewhere. Years later he was

❧❧❧❧❧❧❧❧❧❧❧❧❧❧❧❧❧❧❧❧❧

brought face to face with that Divine intelligence — in the person of Jesus Christ.

It all started when his daughter Rosie and his wife Jean became Christians and began to attend the Elim Church, Keynsham.

Occasionally they would take home audio cassette recordings of my Sunday sermons. I was informed that there was much in my sermons that he did not agree with and would like to discuss with me. This was the open door for me to visit him, which I did — and immediately got involved in a deep and strong discussion on theology. He certainly made it quite clear what he did not believe and pointed out the mistakes, he felt, that I had made.

Although we vigorously disagreed, I liked him and I felt that he warmed towards me — indeed, he invited me to call again; so every now and then I would pay him a visit.

I have fond memories of those visits and the discussions and arguments that ensued. We both enjoyed a good argument and that was the problem; neither would give way to the other.

We discussed God, the Bible, death, Satan, spiritism, evolution, creation etc, in which I would do my best to present the claims of Christ, but from this subject he would shy away.

When in debate or discussion, I always found that George seemed to convey a higher intellectual level; which was hard to penetrate. However, on one occasion, amazingly, he suddenly stated: "Des, you are on a higher level than me, because you are on a spiritual level," — which for someone of the calibre of George Whiting, was quite staggering. I felt something was beginning to happen within him.

A few weeks later, the telephone rang and Rosie was on the line. "Pastor, Dad would like to see you right away — could you come?"

When I arrived at the Whiting home, George was mowing

❦❦❦❦❦❦❦❦❦❦❦❦❦❦❦❦❦❦❦❦❦❦

the lawn. He came over right away and said:

"Pastor, I have something to tell you."

"What is it, George?" I asked.

"The hospital has told me that I have cancer, with only a short time to live — what have you got to say about that?"

I knew that George would like a straight answer, so I replied, "Well, George, I have to say that unless you receive Jesus Christ as your personal Saviour, you are heading to a lost eternity."

"Oh, I thought you would give me a religious answer," said George, with a twinkle in his eye, "but why I've asked to see you is this — I want to be alive for my daughter's wedding. Would you pray that I will be alive for that, as I've written a special speech and I want to be able to deliver it at the reception."

It was an unusual request, but George Whiting was an unusual man; at least he was actually requesting prayer. So there in the garden, on his newly cut lawn, I laid my hand upon his head and asked God to allow him to live for his daughter Rosie's wedding.

We kept up our little visits and he would say, "I'm still alive," — and sure enough, George did live to some months beyond the wedding day. At the reception, standing on a chair, he gave the most skilled, but amazing speech on why he believed in creation and not evolution. All that at his daughter's wedding!

Eventually, George's condition worsened, and one morning Rosie telephoned to say that he had collapsed and the nurses were with him. She also said, "Dad has asked if you would come right away, as he would like to discuss funeral arrangements with you."

"Well, Rosie," I replied, "I normally discuss such things after a person has died, but of course I'll come."

❦❦❦❦❦❦❦❦❦❦❦❦❦❦❦❦❦❦❦❦❦❦

As I drove to the home, I mentally prepared a set of thought-provoking questions for George on his deathbed. I felt, if the process of questions were followed, I might be able to lead George to the Lord.

When I arrived, the nurse was just leaving and the doctor was expected any time. Seizing my opportunity, I entered the room to try and present my 'soul winning' questions; but all George wanted to talk about was his funeral arrangements.

He gave me the service outline, including the hymns, and suggested some things for me to say in my address; and, oh yes — he quietly informed me that he had already paid the funeral director in advance!

Still alone in the room, I tried again to present my well thought-out 'gospel questions' — a last-ditch effort to point him to the Saviour; but he was having none of it.

"I'm too tired for any questions," he retorted. "The nurse has done nothing but ask me questions all morning."

So, with that approach seemingly gone right out of the window — and as a last desperate attempt to home-in on at least *something* spiritual, I made an almost throwaway remark.

"Well George, would you mind if I read a passage from the Bible?" This we had never done in all our previous discussions.

"Oh, alright then," he replied, much to my surprise. I felt he was too tired to keep refusing my requests.

The visit

I read to him Psalm 46, the "God is our refuge and strength" chapter; then John 14, the "many mansions" chapter; plus sections of Revelation 21/22, the "heaven" chapters. After reading these great scriptures, I started to pray, and I must

❦❦❦❦❦❦❦❦❦❦❦❦❦❦❦❦❦❦❦❦

confess that I included in my prayer all the gospel references and statements I could think of — in addition, I prayed the Lord's Prayer and the benediction, plus the verse or two of a hymn. At last, I felt I had to conclude, and say "Amen".

When I prayed the word "Amen", George sighed and said, "Des, the moment you started to read the Bible, Jesus stepped into the room and He is standing over there in that corner right now."

The hair rose on the back of my neck and I felt a wonderful presence. I turned and looked behind me, but saw nothing, — only sensing a Holy presence in the room.

"Des, Jesus is coming closer. He's standing at the foot of the bed. He's looking right at me; those eyes — they're looking right into me."

He then began to describe the face of Christ: "What a beautiful face, what beautiful eyes — so full of love."

George breathed deeply and said with great relief, "I now know Jesus loves me; I now know that when I die, my spirit will go to be with Him — Des, I feel like a little baby inside!"

"That's right George," I said, "you're being born again."

"That's it!" said George with great joy, "I'm being born again!"

At that point, the doctor came, who incidentally was also a Christian. But then I had to leave to allow him to attend to George.

Later, as I was out visiting, the doctor passed me in his car and screeched to a halt.

"Des!" he exclaimed. "What has happened to George?"

There in the middle of the street, through open car windows, I explained as best I could — and we glorified the Lord together.

❀❀❀❀❀❀❀❀❀❀❀❀❀❀❀❀❀❀❀❀❀❀

The following day, I paid George another visit. As soon as I entered the bedroom, I saw that George's face was aglow.

"How is it, George, since you saw Jesus?" I asked.

"Wonderful!" he replied, "I kiss His face every morning." And all I could get out of him were the glories of his 'lovely Saviour'.

"Pastor," said George, "please tell me more about heaven and what it will be like — I can't wait to go there with Jesus."

For the next hour, we shared together the excellencies of the life to come from the scriptures. As we were about to close in prayer, George made a special request; he asked me to pray that when he died, two things would not happen. Apparently the doctor had told him that as he neared his earthly end, he would not be able to drink anything and he would go into a coma.

"Please ask the Lord Jesus that neither of these things will happen when I go to be with Him." This I did.

It was on Easter Monday, 1990, whilst I was in London in the Albert Hall with a coach party from our Keynsham Church, attending an annual Elim National Rally, that George died. I was upset about this, as I wanted to be with him at his departure.

On returning, I asked Jean what his 'home-call' was like.

She replied, "George died peacefully with his family around him. He had not gone into a coma and had been able to sip tea that day."

God had graciously granted his request; during which, suddenly the heavenly chariot was in the room and George Whiting was transported to glory.

❀❀❀❀❀❀❀❀❀❀❀❀❀❀❀❀❀❀❀❀

POSTSCRIPT

Madrid,
9th June 2002
Rosie Cayless

My Memories of Dad's vision of Jesus

"*Dad had always been a very spiritual person, keenly aware of a creative force greater than all mankind and of a supreme intelligence. It was only after seeing a vision of the face of Jesus, however, that Dad really started to talk about Jesus Himself.*

"*Pastor Des came to pray with Dad and read passages from the Bible, relating to death and heaven. During this visit, a vision of Jesus appeared directly in front of Dad. This obviously had a profoundly moving effect, as from then on Dad would talk about Jesus in a deeply affectionate way. I remember him saying that whenever he saw Jesus he would kiss His face, as if the vision had stayed with him.*

"*He also talked lucidly about feeling he was in a rowing boat, rowing towards an island. Jesus was waiting for him on the island, and as he approached, Jesus was going to wade into the water, help Dad ashore and tie up his boat. For me, personally, this is the most reassuring image of death I have ever been presented with.*"

11

Rebecca — miracle baby

Every time a certain pretty young teenager comes to church, I automatically think, "Here comes our miracle girl." Rebecca Reid certainly is an amazing miracle.

When just three weeks old, she was rushed into the Bristol Children's Hospital with the very worst of emergencies — she had stopped breathing!

Due to a vicious respiratory virus, she had been taken desperately ill at home. Her grandmother, Brenda, a qualified midwife, recognising the seriousness of the symptoms, bundled both baby and mother into her car and drove them to the hospital. Unfortunately, it was a journey fraught with panic situations.

On arrival at the hospital, being late at night, Brenda found the emergency entrance door closed. Suddenly, her daughter Rhiannon, who was holding the baby in the car, began to scream — "Mum, she's stopped breathing!"

Brenda took the child in her arms and started to give the kiss of life and also to massage the chest, knowing it was a cardiac arrest.

❧❧❧❧❧❧❧❧❧❧❧❧❧❧❧❧❧❧❧❧❧

Carrying the baby, whilst praying and continuing to massage the heart area, she ran to the side of the hospital building and saw a window just over head height with a light on. Standing on tiptoe, she managed to peer through the window and saw nurses moving about. She called out at the top of her voice and banged on the window — but no one heard or saw her.

With the baby still in her arms, Brenda ran back to the emergency entrance and saw a telephone there, with a number to ring. She desperately dialled the emergency number, waited and watched, but still no one answered. The minutes ticked by. All this time, she was still administering the kiss of life and heart massage. At fever pitch now, Brenda ran back to the high side window and once again tried to attract someone's attention — all to no avail.

Some ten to fifteen minutes had now elapsed since baby Rebecca had stopped breathing, and all hope seemed lost. In utter desperation, she picked up the baby and hoisted her at arm's length in front of the window, crying to God for help.

At that precise moment, a man in the hospital room happened to turn his head and glance up at the window, and caught sight of a baby in a pair of hands. Calling a passing nurse, she in turn looked in astonishment at the uplifted child and Brenda's tear-stained face peering in. As she looked, she saw Brenda mouthing the words: "CARDIAC ARREST."

Immediately the alarm was raised and the medical team flew into action, rushing the baby into intensive care.

The early hours

"Pastor Morton?"

"Yes!"

"Would you come and christen a young baby who is dying in the Children's Hospital, with just a very short time to live?"

❧❧❧❧❧❧❧❧❧❧❧❧❧❧❧❧❧❧❧❧❧

The doctor on the other end of the telephone line had awakened me from a deep sleep at about 3 a.m. Only half awake, I replied, "Doctor, I think you have the wrong minister — we don't christen children, we dedicate them."

"You are Pastor Morton of the Elim Church, Keynsham?"

"Yes."

"Mr and Mrs Reid have asked that you come urgently to the hospital right away — will you come and dedicate their child?"

Wide awake now and realising it was baby Rebecca, daughter of Rhyannon and Ian, I replied, "I'm on my way."

It was the 25th November 1988 and I arrived at the hospital at around 3.45 a.m. The doctor who had telephoned me was waiting for me and, taking me to one side, informed me further of the gravity of the situation. He told me that because of the cardiac arrests, the baby had suffered massive brain damage and was only being kept alive on the ventilator until my arrival, so that I could dedicate the child. He then asked me to persuade the parents to give permission for the life support to be switched off.

Entering the room, I saw the tiny baby in the incubator with Rhyannon and her husband Ian standing anxiously by. The doctor then left us for a short while. I spoke to them and encouraged them to trust in God. Linking hands, we bowed in prayer with the attending nurse also joining in. We asked God to strengthen our faith and prayed the Lord's Prayer together. I then dedicated the baby Rebecca to the Lord Jesus, laid my hands on the incubator and asked for healing in His mighty Name.

The doctor, who had been listening from outside the door, came back into the room and whispered in my ear, reminding me of his request for permission to turn off the life support.

I found myself saying, "Doctor, I've just asked God for a

❧❧❧❧❧❧❧❧❧❧❧❧❧❧❧❧❧❧❧❧❧❧❧

miracle; how can I now ask them to terminate Rebecca's life? I would like more time to see what God will do!"

The doctor sighed, and said, "Alright, we'll wait until tomorrow. I'm going home to sleep now, I'll be back at 12 noon."

"That's fine," I replied, "I'll see you here then."

When I returned home at around 5 a.m., Rosalie, my wife, was waiting for me with astonishing news.

"Des — I had a vision of baby Rebecca while you were gone. I was praying and in my mind I saw the baby die — it was as clear as crystal; then I saw her alive again — but that's not all, I also saw her as a grown child. I believe God is going to work a miracle."

With this encouraging announcement ringing in my ears, I went back to bed and snatched a couple of hours' sleep.

At 12 noon, I returned to the Children's Hospital and found the doctor, once again waiting for me. He was very forthright this time:

"Mr Morton, I really must ask you to prevail upon the parents to grant permission for the life support to be turned off."

He explained that although the child had not worsened in the night, she still had massive brain damage and would not live anyway. He also added that Rhyannon and Ian had gone home for a shower and change of clothes and would be back shortly.

Seizing the opportunity of a further brief time gap, I retorted, "Doctor, I would like to pray for the baby again!"

"She still has brain damage," he replied firmly.

"Maybe — but may I tell you a true story?"

"What's that?" he said.

"Doctor, what happened to baby Rebecca, happened to my brother a few years ago."

❧❧❧❧❧❧❧❧❧❧❧❧❧❧❧❧❧❧❧❧❧❧❧

I proceeded to tell him what happened to my brother Leslie, when his heart stopped twice and was starved of oxygen to the brain for a long period of time. How the doctor at Frenchay Hospital had told me exactly the same thing, that there was no hope, but after prayer he had made a full recovery. I told him that prayer *does* change things and that lots of Christian people were now praying for this child and I would like another chance to pray over the incubator.

The doctor looked at me rather directly, then nodded and said, "Well I suppose you had better pray for her again — and we'll wait and see."

So, once again, I prayed over the child, asking the Lord to intervene and meet the need.

It begins

Throughout the rest of the day, there was very little change, but she grew no worse. Her parents, who had returned to her side, just sat by, gently stroking her arms and hands. The following day, there was a slight improvement; then suddenly, whilst still in the incubator, she began to breathe by herself. The miraculous had begun. Her mother was allowed to feed her and the following day she was moved to a side ward. From that point on, her recovery was rapid. The consultant's own words were: **"She truly is a miracle."**

Over the ensuing month, Rebecca had brain scans and many tests, but at the conclusion was pronounced 100% normal and fit, without a trace of brain damage.

One year later, at Christmas 1989, she saw the same consultant for a check-up, but he completely discharged her, saying, "I would dearly love to see her again, but I don't have a good enough excuse!"

Today, Rebecca is a healthy, intelligent young teenager, doing well at school, is a keen ballet dancer and is often seen using her skills in youth presentations at the church.

"His touch has still its ancient power."

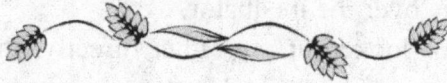

12

Angel

One night, six weeks before Christmas 1985, I suddenly awoke from a deep sleep. Opening my eyes, I was startled to see a young man standing at the foot of the bed. He looked about thirty years of age and over six feet tall. His hair was golden and flowed back down to his shoulders in old Anglo-Saxon style, having a parting in the middle. His face was the most beautiful face I had ever seen on a young man, with perfectly chiselled features.

He wore a very simple, plain white tunic with short sleeves and thonged at the neck. He was extremely well built and muscular. His whole being glowed in the darkness with a soft blue light that radiated from him. He just stood there, at the foot of the bed — watching!

My wife was still asleep by the side of me; however, I noticed that he was not actually looking at us, but watching over us. In fact, he was peering at the bedroom door to our left. Apparently, something had caught his attention, and he just stood there – watching! Instinctively, I knew that I was observing an angel from heaven.

CHAPTER TWELVE

The thing that impressed me at the time was that I was not the least bit afraid. I had always thought that if ever I saw an angel, I would be struck with fear like so many in the Bible. However, I can only say that to me, it seemed the most natural thing in the world, and I tingled with excitement as I gazed at his appearance.

Probably the whole experience lasted no more than four or five minutes, but it seemed longer. I remember pinching myself to make sure that I wasn't dreaming and also turning to look at Rosalie who was still fast asleep.

The angel seemed completely unaware that I could see him and was intently observing him. The thought that entered my mind was: 'What next?' Should I say something, or wait for him to make the first move? I decided to take the bull by the horns and speak to him.

With that decision made, I pushed myself up on my elbows and was just about to say, "Good evening, it's good to see you," when he noticed my sudden movement, looked startled and disappeared before my eyes.

Extremely disappointed, I sank back between the sheets and just lay there contemplating what had just happened. I remained wide awake for over an hour hoping the heavenly visitor might put in another appearance, but nothing further happened and I drifted off to sleep again.

For three days, I kept the visitation a secret, but on the fourth day, decided to break the news to Rosalie. I had wondered how the supernatural occurrence might affect my family, so I was slow to reveal it. However, I need not have worried; Rosalie was absolutely thrilled.

"Des," she replied, "do you realise that you have been allowed to see our guardian angel, the one who watches over us?"

Later, we broke the news to our son David, and to our

70

🌸🌸🌸🌸🌸🌸🌸🌸🌸🌸🌸🌸🌸🌸🌸🌸🌸🌸🌸🌸🌸

young nephew, Kevin, who was living with us at the time. They also, were thrilled and excited and began to refer to the heavenly visitor as 'our angel'.

ANGELS

The Bible teaches that angelic appearances are always for a particular purpose; so I began to wonder why it was that God had allowed this visitation as He had. It certainly was an amazing stepping-stone experience for me; indeed, it led me straight away into several important areas.

Firstly, it radically opened my mind to the reality of the spirit world around us, just beyond our natural sight.

Secondly, I saw that angels were indeed 'ministering spirits' working on our behalf (Hebrews 1:14). That November night, I had encountered such a personage in our house, but I think on this occasion, he was as surprised as I was.

Thirdly, this angelic revelation triggered within me a hunger for information concerning such wonderful beings, and it drove me to the scriptures.

I spent many weeks studying what the Bible taught on 'The Miraculous Ministry of Angels'. Indeed this became the title of a weekly series of Bible studies that developed so that I presented and taught them at the church. Every now and then I still preach on the subject, being still gripped with the occasion of that event.

The unfolding truth from the scriptures informed me that angels are real created spirit beings, innumerable; powerful; joyful; wise; intelligent and of great age — indeed, they witnessed the creation of the universe (Job 38:4-7).

The Bible also reveals that angels are celestial powers of differing rank, authority and employment, operating a divine

❧❧❧❧❧❧❧❧❧❧❧❧❧❧❧❧❧❧❧❧❧

messenger and surveillance service between heaven and earth (Luke 1:19); (Daniel 4:13).

For some reason, known only to God, I was allowed to catch a brief glimpse of one such angel on duty, in our bedroom. The thrill of that glimpse remains with me to this day.

Glow

The main service of angels is, of course, the worship of Almighty God around the throne. It would seem logical that one effect of journeyings to and fro from the great throne room of heaven, would be to bring something of that heavenly glory with them. The Apostle John, when describing his vision of the Holy City, 'New Jerusalem', spoke of it as shining with "the glory of God; and its brilliance was like that of a very precious jewel, like a jasper, clear as crystal" (Revelation 21:11).

Jasper is translucent quartz and one of its colours, along with other colour tints, is sky blue. (Unger's Bible Dictionary, mineral section.) Could this account for the bright bluish glow that radiated from my visiting angel? Did he bring something of the colour of heaven with him? I've often wondered why blue is my favourite colour.

Latter days

The Bible indicates that in the last days before Christ returns, there is going to be a lot more angelic activity and visitation to earth. Indeed, during the actual coming of Christ, millions of angels will accompany the Son of God back to earth in spectacular manner — but that is the subject of our next chapter.

❧❧❧❧❧❧❧❧❧❧❧❧❧❧❧❧❧❧❧❧❧

13

Into the future

One afternoon in 1956, I boarded a bus at the Bristol City Centre, after visiting the nearby local Bible shop in Park Street. I was 23 years of age and had been a Christian for just a few short months. A deep hunger for the Word of God had already settled upon my heart and that was the reason why I had just spent the previous hour browsing through some of the great study books and commentaries on the shelves of the bookshop.

With my mind thinking about 'books' and wondering which ones to save up for, I clambered aboard the double-decker bus and took my seat on the upper deck.

As I gazed out of the bus window onto the people and traffic below, I gradually became aware of the presence of God coming upon me. Turning to look down the bus gangway, the anointing grew stronger and suddenly a vision of blue skies and white clouds appeared before my eyes. Then came the vivid shock of seeing the massive sky filled with thousands upon thousands of riders, all astride white horses, rushing toward planet earth. All the riders wore gleaming white garments; and out in front, leading this cavalry invasion was Jesus Christ, wearing a glittering crown and Himself seated upon a magnificent white charger.

❦❦❦❦❦❦❦❦❦❦❦❦❦❦❦❦❦❦❦❦❦❦

Thrilling though the vision was, it lasted only a few seconds and then was gone; but it was indelibly printed upon my mind and spirit. At the time, I knew very little about the prophetic truth of Christ's second coming to earth, but from that moment, I was determined to know more. The section of the Lord's Prayer, "Thy Kingdom come" took on new meaning and purpose for me as I set myself the task of studying this great Bible truth. (See Appendix.)

For the past forty-seven years, I have been a student of Bible prophecy, driven by the initial 'vision' received that day on the number 8 bus. My studies have been like a bus journey of discovery, stopping at different stages of prophetic truth along the way.

For example, I discovered that my momentary visualisation of the Second Advent was in fact, the coming 'Revelation' of Christ at the great and terrible battle of Armageddon.

This would take place when the Jerusalem of the last days would be besieged on either side by the armies of many nations; then at the zenith of the battle, when it seemed as if the city would be no more, Jesus 'The Messiah' appears with His mighty heavenly armies of saints and angels. His coming, with power and great glory, delivers Israel and devastates her enemies. He is revealed as 'King of Kings' and 'Lord of Lords'; sets His Kingdom up on earth; ruling and reigning for a thousand years — termed the 'millennial reign of Christ'.

All this would be preceded by 'The Rapture' (the catching away of the Church) — some seven years earlier. The Apostle Paul declared of that momentous occasion:

"The Lord Himself will come down from heaven, with a loud command, with the voice of the archangel and with the trumpet call of God; and the dead in Christ will rise first. After that, we who are still alive and are left will be caught up together with them in the clouds, to meet the Lord in the air.

❧❧❧❧❧❧❧❧❧❧❧❧❧❧❧❧❧❧❧❧❧

And so we will be with the Lord for ever. Therefore encourage each other with these words." (1Thessalonians 4:16-18.)

At the sound of Christ's voice (which only Christians will hear), the dead in Christ will be resurrected and all living believers will suddenly disappear from the earth, caught up to meet the Lord Jesus in the air.

The remainder will be left behind to face a world vacated by the Church, in a terrible period called the 'Great Tribulation'. Lasting seven years, this tribulation time period (also called Daniel's 70th week), starts with the rapture and ends with the Revelation of Christ — the vision that I saw!

Many Christians believe that the rapture of the Church could take place very soon. The reason for this expectation is the amazing fulfilment of Bible prophecies in our day and generation. Jesus called them 'signs of the times' (Matthew 16:3).

There are many such prophetic signs unfolding daily around us, including:
- Wars and rumours of wars
- Catastrophic famines
- Devastating earthquakes
- Freak convulsions of nature
- Global distress and terror, etc

But the major sign is the nation of Israel itself! The return of the Jews to Israel (1948) and their ancient capital, Jerusalem (1967), are the greatest prophetic fulfilments of our time. Jesus clearly pointed out that the generation that saw this would be the final generation that would witness His coming (Luke 21:20-28).

There is no doubt about it. We are living in amazing days — last days that will soon see the coming of the Lord. He is coming to receive to Himself His glorious Church and then to reign in power and glory here on earth.

Such a glorious event, however, will in itself be but a

further stepping-stone to many other glorious and thrilling events yet to unfold — "stepping-stones" into the wonderful developing destiny, laid up for all those who love Him. But that is another story.

CONCLUSION

Jesus said, "My Father is working still" (John 5:17 RSV).

God is at work! — Sometimes working visibly and dramatically, and at other times, invisibly and behind the scenes. What often appears to be sheer coincidence is God's Divine engineering! Indeed, someone has described 'coincidence' as 'a miracle where God prefers to remain anonymous'. It is only later, that we discover His hand in it all.

Once, years ago, my wife Rosalie took our two-year-old son, David, on a bus journey to visit her mother. She wheeled him to the local bus stop in a small pushchair. Whilst waiting for the bus, she got into a brief conversation with another young mother named Sandra, and for just a few minutes got into 'mums talk' before their bus arrived. Later, when Rosalie arrived at her mother's home, she realised that the pushchair apron was missing. Presuming that she had left it on the bus, she made enquiries, but all to no avail. It was lost.

The very next day, Rosalie opened our house front door and there, standing in the road right outside, was Sandra, with the lost pushchair apron in her hand.

"Rosalie," she said smilingly, "your apron fell into my pushchair."

Apparently, at the bus stop, Sandra heard Rosalie mention

the name of the road where we lived and decided to try and find us. She was actually walking down the road, wondering which house to knock at, when Rosalie suddenly opened the front door and stared wide-eyed into Sandra's smiling face. Rosalie invited her in for a cup of tea, the first of many such invitations; and in the process of time, Sandra gave her heart to the Lord Jesus Christ.

Later, Sandra asked me if I would visit her dying mother and pray for her. This I did the following day, and finding her mother lying on a couch in the lounge, I knelt down by her side and explained the simple message of the gospel. Within minutes, I had the joy of leading the dear woman to Christ. She prayed with me the sinner's prayer of commitment and gratefully received the Lord Jesus as her personal Saviour.

Unknown to me, the lounge door was a little ajar and standing outside listening to all that was being said, was the woman's sister. After I had finished praying, the sister entered the room with tears in her eyes, to say that she also had prayed the prayer of commitment at the very same time and had received Christ as her Saviour.

The chain of miracles, however, did not stop there; for, because of Sandra's frequent visits to our house, a regular weekly coffee morning started with other young mums attending from the area. This continued for many weeks, resulting in a number surrendering their lives to Christ, one of whom was a Jehovah's Witness.

Truly, the ways of God are past finding out. He who used Moses' 'rod'; David's 'sling-shot' and a small boy's 'lunch' of five loaves and two fishes, also saw fit to use Rosalie's pushchair 'apron' for His glory!

The loving Heavenly Father is continually working behind the scenes in miracle power, and what can seem to be an insignificant occurrence, can often be the 'finger of God'.

Indeed, what sometimes can be an apparent tragedy, again, can be the outworking of God. When Joseph, the favourite son of Jacob, was sold into slavery by his jealous scheming brothers, little did he or anyone else know that it was part of God's great plan for the development of the nation of Israel, forged in the land of Egypt. When at last Joseph was exalted to his position of great power and authority in Egypt, next to Pharaoh himself, he was able to turn to his frightened brothers, who were trembling before him, and say:

"I am your brother Joseph, the one you sold into Egypt! And now, do not be distressed and do not be angry with yourselves for selling me here, because it was to save lives that God sent me ahead of you." (Genesis 45:4b,5.)

God did it — it was all part of His plan to save and preserve them. It certainly did not seem like it at the time, but God was working it all out for Joseph's good — and his family's good also.

All things

The wonderful truth is, that God has not changed (Malachi 3:6), and He is still shaping and re-shaping things for our benefit.

The Apostle Paul wrote: *"And we know that in all things God works for the good of those who love Him, who have been called according to His purpose."* (Romans 8:28.)

'All things' means the bad things as well as the good things. Sometimes, when you go to a pharmacist for a prescribed medicine, the chemist will perhaps mix a poison with other drugs to fight the poison of the disease. He uses what normally is considered a 'bad' thing for the patient's good. God in His perfect all-knowledge, sometimes does just that, working 'all things', even the 'bad things', out for our good.

God is at work at all times in our lives — always on our behalf, because He loves us, and has a plan for us. He says: *"For I know the plans I have for you," declares the Lord, "plans to prosper you and not to harm you, plans to give you hope and a future."* (Jeremiah 29:11.)

God is in us, with us and for us; and He is continually working it all out for our good. He is always on the job. Our "Father is working still". It is stepping-stone miracles all the way, even when we do not realise it.

APPENDIX

Three questions people ask.

1.

"If there is a God,
why does He allow suffering?"

This is a question I was asked recently by some young mothers, at our church 'Mums and Toddlers' group. I find this to be one of the most pressing questions of our time. More pressing than such questions as: "Did we all come from monkeys?" "Is there life after death?" or "When will the world end?"

It is more deeply rooted than any other question, because it deals with the classic problem of God Himself. It indeed raises the question, whether there is a God at all? Or, if there is a God, is He all-powerful but not all good? Or, is He all good but unable to control evil? — In which case, He would not be all-powerful.

The question is certainly a very complex one.

Why?

Dr Billy Graham, the international evangelist, in his message at the American National Day of Prayer and Remembrance, Friday September 14th 2001 — just three days after the Twin Towers catastrophe, said:

"I have been asked hundreds of times why God allows tragedy and suffering. I have to confess that I really do not know the answer totally, even to my own satisfaction. I have to accept by faith, that God is sovereign and He is a God of love and mercy and compassion in the midst of suffering."

I have to agree with Dr Graham. It is a question perhaps only God Himself can fully answer, because of its profundity. However, the Bible does teach that suffering and death are in the world because of three basic reasons:

• BECAUSE OF SIN.

Sin is the great blot upon humanity. Sin is the transgression of God's Holy law and is rebellion against Him. Sin is something we all have committed, the result of which is death.

"All have sinned and fall short of the glory of God." (Romans 3:23);

"Therefore, just as sin entered the world through one man, and death through sin, and in this way death came to all men, because all sinned —" (Romans 5:12);

"The wages of sin is death" (Romans 6:23).

Death, (also sickness and suffering which precede death) is a direct result of sin. Every sick bed, funeral and heartache, is an offshoot of man's universal rebellion against God.

The second great cause of suffering in the world is:

• MAN HIMSELF.

All the wars, murders, attacks and strife of all ages, have stemmed from man's greed, lust, hate and pride. Many of the great disasters of humanity, such as rail and plane crashes, are often down to man's neglect or imperfections.

This was the case in the catastrophic Aberfan tragedy of the 1960s, when a sliding mountain of coal slag enveloped a school, killing all inside.

A third great cause of suffering in the world today is:

❧❧❧❧❧❧❧❧❧❧❧❧❧❧❧❧❧❧❧❧❧❧

• THE DEVIL.

The fact is, that man is not alone on planet earth. The Bible teaches of the presence of an evil enemy of mankind. He comes against humanity as a tempting 'angel of light' on the one hand, and as a 'destroying roaring lion' on the other. Jesus called him 'Satan' — the devil!

Every one of us can detect that there are two powers at work in the world around us — the power for good, and the power for evil. They flow like two mighty rivers through life.

All rivers have a source. The Bible teaches that all good comes from God and all evil comes from Satan — the evil one. Satan is the originator of sin. The Bible calls him the father of liars and a murderer from the beginning (John 8:44). It also labels him the tempter and deceiver of men. (Matt. 4:3; Rev. 12:9.)

The root cause of sin and temptation is therefore the devil himself. Without his deceptions, man would not be tempted in the first place.

Sickness, suffering and death, are in reality knock-on effects of sin, brought about by the tempter. Such terrible experiences are root works of Satan. It is he who is at the back of it all. He finds great satisfaction in endeavouring to ruin God's creation — causing misery and suffering in his wake. The awful tragedy of September 11th, 2001, tells us that there is indeed an evil presence at work in this world.

Action

The question may be asked, "WHY DOESN'T GOD DO SOMETHING ABOUT IT?" The answer is twofold:
FIRST — God already *has* done something.
Two thousand years ago, He sent His only begotten Son, Jesus

Christ, to redeem us. He did this by paying the full price for our sins upon the cross of Calvary, so that we might be forgiven. (John 3:16; 1 Peter 2:24; Ephesians 1:7.)

SECOND — He will yet intervene and with the final provision for this world's needs.

The Bible tells us, that one day soon, in these last days of time, almighty God will send His Son to earth a second time. Christ will come again as King of Kings and Lord of Lords. At His coming, evil will be arrested and peace will reign. (John 14:1-3; 1 Thessalonians 4:13-18; Revelation 19:11-16; Zechariah 14.)

What must be realised, however, is that in the midst of all suffering — God, Himself, is the great sufferer.

As we survey the wondrous cross, we realise that God Himself suffered terribly in the sacrifice of His Son — *"God was in Christ, reconciling the world to Himself"* (2 Corinthians 5:19 [KJV]). He knows all about suffering, and the scripture tells us He is touched with the pain of our infirmities. When we suffer, He feels it and understands.

Iron cross

This great truth was graphically brought home two days after the terrorist attack on New York when the twin towers of the World Trade Centre collapsed. Workers unearthed a 20-foot cast iron cross among the rubble. A huge cross, consisting of two metal girders, fell like a giant spear into the ruins. After the uncannily shaped beams were found, the workers hoisted the cross to a special foundation to be seen by passers-by.

Groups of firefighters, police and construction workers gathered to pray at the cross. A Minister, Rev. Brian Jordon,

❧❧❧❧❧❧❧❧❧❧❧❧❧❧❧❧❧❧❧❧❧

also prayed with the workers and said, *"Behold the glory of the cross at ground level"*.

Nothing could be more descriptive. This giant ugly cross somehow conveyed the suffering of God Himself at 'Ground Zero'; that He too, felt the suffering of that terrible day and put His mark there.

The cross of Christ clearly conveys the awesome fact that God Himself is the great sufferer, and has fully met the problem of sin and evil in the gift of His only Son — at infinite cost to Himself.

God never asks us to understand the great mysteries of suffering; only to trust Him. Becoming a Christian does not make us immune from the tragedies of life, but He does promise to be with us every step of the way. He also promises that one day, all questions will be answered and when we see Him, we will understand 'WHY?'

Have you ever seen someone working on a tapestry or embroidery? The side that you see being worked upon, is often an ugly tangle of knots and ends; but when the finished article is turned over, you see the full beautiful picture.

One day, we shall see things from the other side. We will see as God sees and view the full beautiful plan with perfect understanding.

Assurance

One thing we are assured of in Scripture, is that a glorious time is approaching for all true believers in Christ — when all tears will be wiped away and all suffering eradicated.

The Apostle John said: *"I saw the Holy City, the new Jerusalem, coming down out of heaven from God, prepared as a bride beautifully dressed for her husband. And I heard a loud voice from the throne saying, 'Now the dwelling of God is*

with men, and He will live with them. They will be His people and God Himself will be with them and be their God. He will wipe every tear from their eyes. There will be no more death or mourning or crying or pain, for the old order of things has passed away'." (Revelation 21:2-4.) Christians do not pass away — only death, sorrow, tears and pain pass away! Christians pass into the wonderful destiny laid up for them by the Lord Jesus Christ. To every believer He says: — *"I am going there to prepare a place for you"* (John 14:2).

Christians know and understand that the complete answer to life's most pressing problems is ***JESUS CHRIST!***

2.

"Will Jesus come to earth again?"

What if Jesus came back to earth tomorrow? The whole world would be in for a terrific shock. One can only imagine the chain reaction of effects that would follow. Christ's second coming would cause thrones to topple, governments to fall and wars to cease. World powers would immediately submit to the theocratic rule of the Kings of Kings. Atheists would fearfully admit their utter folly before the Almighty God. Red-faced liberal theologians would feverishly chase through ancient Biblical prophecies previously discounted. Weeping Christian backsliders would bow their heads in shame before the sad gaze of their Lord. Followers of false religions would have to face up to the shattering fact that they were deluded by false prophets and evil doctrines, and would have to confront the true God. Even some committed Christians would be shaken and surprised by this event, because they were not looking for His coming. It is amazing to discover just how many lovely followers of Christ possess so little knowledge of Christ's second advent.

The fact is, according to Scripture, Jesus Christ could return at any time, because the Bible proclaims an imminent coming: James 5:8, Hebrews 10:25. The Bible warns believers not to sleep as others do, but to watch, in case that day of Christ's coming should overtake them as a thief in the night (1 Thessalonians 5:6).

❧❧❧❧❧❧❧❧❧❧❧❧❧❧❧❧❧❧❧❧❧❧

Coming King

Bible students know that the flipside of Christmas is the second coming of Jesus Christ. Two thousand years ago, the Son of God visited this planet earth as a tiny babe, and prophecy declares that He will one day return in spectacular magnificence as King of Kings and Lord of Lords. Over three hundred times in the New Testament alone, mention is made of this glorious second advent.

In the historical past, angels, prophets and apostles stood on tip-toe peering into the revealed future, pointing towards this tremendous event. They saw the coming Saviour crowned with glory and honour, descending with the shining armies of heaven. They viewed the open skies, filled with raptured saints and mighty angels. They surveyed the winding up of the ages with the judgement of the nations. They envisaged a changing world, becoming heaven on earth, because the Kingdom of God had come. They spied the binding of Satan, and the bowing of every knee to the exalted Name of Jesus. All this they saw through the Spirit of prophecy, in what was then the distant future. All this we now see, as foretold in the Bible, is now our near future. The whole situation has now moved dramatically closer.

Signs and times

Many Christians believe that Christ's second appearing could take place very soon. The reason for this expectation is the amazing fulfilment of Bible prophecies in our day. Jesus called prophetic fulfilments: "signs of the times". There are many such signs foretold in Scripture. The gospels alone bristle with them. Jesus was asked by His followers for the signs of His coming again, and of the end of the age. In Matthew 24 and Luke 21, He replied, by listing 12 of them. Jesus concluded His discourse on the end time signs, by saying ... *"When these things begin totake place, stand up and lift up your heads, because your redemption is drawing near."* (Luke 21:28.)

Many of "these things" have already begun to emerge, like the first green buds of springtime.

Rapture and Revelation

The coming of the Lord is one glorious event, but divided into two stages. Like the two sides of a coin, they are part of the whole.

The Rapture, or catching away of the church from the earth, takes place in the first stage, when Christ comes for His people (2 Thessalonians 2:1).

The Revelation, or appearing and actual coming of the Lord to earth, occurs when He returns with His people to rule and reign.

The climax is reached at the battle of Armageddon, the final war of the age. Armageddon is the Hebrew name given to a huge stretch of land in the vale of Megiddo, situated to the north of Jerusalem in Israel. Here armies from many nations will be arrayed in battle against Israel; and when the siege of Jerusalem is at its height, the skies will part and Christ will appear with the armies of Heaven.

The very brightness of His sudden revelation will destroy the forces that fight His ancient people. He will descend with all His saints and His feet will stand once again on the Mount of Olives. The Jews will look upon Jesus whom they crucified, and realise Him to be their true Messiah, and will worship

🌱🌱🌱🌱🌱🌱🌱🌱🌱🌱🌱🌱🌱🌱🌱🌱🌱🌱🌱🌱🌱

Him.

Christ, as King of Kings and Lord of Lords, will enter Jerusalem, sit upon the throne of David, and rule this planet in righteousness. The revealing of the Son of God from Heaven will usher in a millennium of true peace on earth, because the "Prince of Peace" will have come (Revelation 16:16, 19:11-21).

Prophetic proof

When Frederick the Great asked his court preacher for an unanswerable proof of the inspiration of the Bible, he replied: "Your Majesty — the Jew." The Jews are the most amazing people under the sun. They have survived 1900 years of the most bitter slavery, slaughter and persecution and yet remained a nation without a country. Normally, under such conditions, such a people would eventually lose their national identity. The Jews, however, remained a nation without a country over many centuries. There are German Jews, American Jews, Russian Jews, English Jews, even Chinese Jews. Their existence and identity is a miracle.

"The return of the Jews to Israel and their ancient capital, is the greatest prophetic event of our time."

During World War Two, my old Methodist grandfather would say that one day, according to prophecy, the Jews would return to Palestine (Ezekiel 37:21). At the time, such an event seemed far from possible. Just a few years later, however, as a result of the war and other international factions, hundreds of thousands of Jews began to return to their ancient homeland. In 1948 the state of Israel was formed, and later in 1967, after the amazing six day war, the old city of Jerusalem was occupied. Today, Israel is one of the most powerful nations in the Middle East, with a thriving population of over three million Jews.

The return of the Jews to Israel and their ancient capital is the greatest prophetic event of our time. David Ben Gurion, the late Prime Minister of Israel, said: "Whether my people believe it or not, they are returning to their land in order to herald the coming of the Messiah."

Twenty-one times our Lord Himself said He would come again. He taught that the presence of the Jews in Jerusalem would pinpoint the generation in which He would return (Luke 21:25-32).

The Jews will have to return to their land in large numbers, for the prophesied tribulation time to unfold. This they have already done, in our generation. How near then must be the rapture? This Jewish situation which pin-points the last generation, is the hub in a whole wheel of international occurrence.

The E.C.; Russia and Red China; the World Council of Churches; New Age Movement, and resurgence of Islam, are all part of the prophetic picture. Like pieces of a giant jig-saw puzzle, they are coming together on the table of prophecy, as if moved by invisible hands.

Ready or not ready?

The signs of the times clearly indicate that the coming of the Lord for His Church is now drawing very near, and is the next major event on God's prophetic calendar. The Bible teaches that only those who have received Christ as Saviour will be truly ready; His coming being the completeness of their salvation (John 1:12, Romans 13:11).

❧❧❧❧❧❧❧❧❧❧❧❧❧❧❧❧❧❧❧❧❧❧

Check these prophecies for yourself:

Matthew 24 and Luke 21

1. The emergence of false Christs
2. Wars and rumours of wars
3. Catastrophic famines
4. Rampant disease
5. Great earthquakes
6. Anti-Semitism
7. False prophets
8. Worldwide evangelism
9. The end of Gentile rule in Israel
10. Unusual phenomena in outer space
11. Global distress and terror
12. Freak convulsions of nature.

3

"What is a Christian?"

A man called David Otis Fuller once asked the penetrating question: "If you were ever arrested for being a Christian would there be enough evidence to convict you?"[1]

Such a question raises the further question: "What is a Christian?"

The word 'Christian' appears only three times in the Bible but today it is used more than any other term to describe a follower of Jesus Christ.

It was first given as a nickname and not a very complimentary one at that.

Indeed, when it was used, it was spoken as a form of abuse, linking the disciples with the Galilean troublemaker called Jesus, who was executed among thieves on a Roman cross.

It was a name spat out by many, and considered to be the lowest form of reproach. The Roman historian Tacitus wrote of those "populous, or common people called Christians".

Gradually however, something wonderful began to happen. The early disciples used this derogatory nickname; they took the mud slung at them.

❧❧❧❧❧❧❧❧❧❧❧❧❧❧❧❧❧❧❧❧❧

They fashioned the name into a badge of honour. Soon it became the noblest title of all.

Today, there is no better name to describe one who follows Jesus Christ, and trusts in Him as Saviour and Lord. A Christian is a "Christ-one".

Decision

It must be said that a person is not automatically a Christian because he or she is born in a Christian country, or brought up in a religious home.

An individual becomes a Christian through personal choice. A decision must be made involving repentance and faith. The Bible calls it conversion.

Recently, a young teenager came to me after the Sunday night service, and said that she had asked Christ into her life, and decided to follow Him. I rejoiced at her confession, and was able to tell her that, in my opinion, she had done the best and wisest thing she would ever do.

Often, I read and hear of people who, as they come to the end of their earthly journey, confess with deep sorrow the things they have done in life, but I have never heard anyone on their death bed confess: "I am sorry I was a Christian. I am sorry I followed Jesus Christ."

It has been said: "Faith makes a Christian; Life proves a Christian; Trial confirms a Christian; Death crowns a Christian".

Heaven open

As old-time evangelist D. L. Moody lay dying, surrounded by relatives and friends, he suddenly awoke from a peaceful sleep and in slow measured tones, said, "Earth

❀❀❀❀❀❀❀❀❀❀❀❀❀❀❀❀❀❀❀❀❀❀

recedes, Heaven opens before me — if this is death it is sweet. God is calling me and I must go."[2]

Some time later, he closed his eyes and was gone. Why did he see Heaven open before him at the time of death? The answer is very simple; as a young man he believed on Jesus as his personal Saviour and followed Him through life and into eternity.

> *"For God so loved the world, that He gave His only*
> *begotten Son, that whoever believes in Him*
> *should not perish, but have everlasting life."*
> *John 3:16 (NKJV)*

NOTES

Appendix — 3. "What is a Christian?"

1. John Blanchard, *Gathered Gold*.

2. John Pollock, *Moody Without Sankey*.

PERMISSION ACKNOWLEDGEMENTS

Leslie Morton
Sheila Anderson
Graham and Marilyn Britton
Jean Whiting
Rosie Cayless
Rhiannon Reid
Brenda Williams

BIBLIOGRAPHY

Blanchard, John: 'Gathered Gold', Evangelical Press.
Pollock, John: 'Moody Without Sankey', Hodder & Stoughton.